# EVERYDAY CHALLENGES

## ACTIVITY PACK

supporting the *SEN Press* 'Everyday Challenges' series ...

WWW.SENPRESS.CO.UK

## Introduction

# ABOUT SEN PRESS

Since its launch in June 2006, *SEN Press* has quickly established itself in the field of special needs education. Concentrating initially on the 'transition' years (14-19), and the twin fields of Life Skills and Literacy, it now has a wide range of appropriate readers available that support ASDAN and other established Life Skills and Social Skills courses.

*SEN Press* is currently developing a set of Activity Packs (interactive CDs with Teacher Notes) to accompany each series of books. The *Work Experience* resources are already available.

All resources may be viewed and ordered through our website: **www.senpress.co.uk**

The publisher's founder and owner, Peter Clarke, has taught for twenty years in the fields of literacy and special education. He has also had first-hand experience of bringing up his Down's Syndrome son, Adam, who, thanks to an excellent education, is now able to hold down a simple, unpaid job and travel independently on the bus.

*SEN Press* publications are endorsed by ASDAN
www.asdan.co.uk

browse and order at
## www.senpress.co.uk

**Phone** 01422 844822
**Email** peterclarke@senpress.co.uk
**Address** 7 Cliffe Street, Hebden Bridge, West Yorkshire HX7 8BY

**Everyday Challenges Activity Pack**
Published: September 2008.
ISBN: 978-1-905579-56-3 © SEN Press 2008
A CIP record of this publication is available from the British Library.
(Schools are free to photocopy materials in this publication for use in class or for homework.)

## SITE LICENCE INCLUDED

**Minimum PC system requirements to run the interactive CD-ROM are:**
Pentium II 600 Mhz
128 Mb RAM
16x CD-ROM drive
16 bit colour display

**Minimum Mac system requirements to run the interactive CD-ROM are:**
G3 Processor or higher
Mac OSX 10.1.5 or higher
256MB RAM
16-bit Color
16-bit sound card
16x CD-ROM

### ACKNOWLEDGEMENTS

I have received a lot of help in developing the *Everyday Challenges* books and the Activity Pack, so my thanks go to :

Ian Hunt, Duncan Witham, Shaun Rafferty and Joe Butcher at *Q&D Multimedia* in Derby

Catherine Burch, my book editor at *Cambridge Publishing Management*

Janie Nicholas: marketing consultant, activity pack editor

Special Needs teachers: Kelso Peel and Christine Richardson (Rochdale), Jayne Cowdale (Wolverhampton), Sophia England (London) and Neil Mears (Chessington, Surrey).

Heather Fry at *ASDAN* in Bristol

Authors and illustrators of this series: Bob Moulder, Sarah Wimperis, Jean de Lemos (*Graham-Cameron Illustration Agency*); Mike Lacey (*SGA Agency*); Lyn Knott (*Sylvie Poggio Agency*) and author Sue Graves (author).

*Peter Clarke, Publisher*

# CONTENTS

## 1. INTRODUCTION

| | |
|---|---|
| About *SEN Press* | *i* |
| Contents | *ii* |
| Preface | *iii* |
| How to install the CD-ROM | *iii* |
| About these Resources: | |
| - The CD-ROM | *iv* |
| - The Teacher Book | *iv* |
| - The 'Everyday Challenges' reading books and where to buy them | *iv* |
| - The Interactive Activities | *v* |
| - The Resource Sheets | *vi* |
| Key buttons and icons in the Interactive Activities | *vii-ix* |
| Lesson Planning: suggestions for using the Activity Pack | *x* |
| Reading Ages | *x* |
| Generic 'What is a Challenge?' / 'Ready for a Challenge' Interactive Activity | *xi* |
| Generic 'My Challenges' worksheet | *xii* |

## 2. TRAVELLING BY YOURSELF

| | |
|---|---|
| The book | 1 |
| Page-by-page notes | 2-4 |
| Interactive Activities | 5-10 |
| Resource Sheets | 11-20 |

## 3. MOVING ON TO COLLEGE

| | |
|---|---|
| The book | 21 |
| Page-by-page notes | 22-23 |
| Interactive Activities | 24-26 |
| Resource Sheets | 27-37 |

## 4. SWIMMING A LENGTH

| | |
|---|---|
| The book | 38 |
| Page-by-page notes | 39-40 |
| Interactive Activities | 41-42 |
| Resource Sheets | 43-53 |

## 5. LEARNING TO SPEAK UP

| | |
|---|---|
| The book | 54 |
| Page-by-page notes | 55-56 |
| Interactive Activities | 57-58 |
| Resource Sheets | 59-69 |

## 6. SHOPPING FOR MUM

| | |
|---|---|
| The book | 70 |
| Page-by-page notes | 71-72 |
| Interactive Activities | 73-74 |
| Resource Sheets | 75-85 |

## 7. SHOPPING FOR CLOTHES

| | |
|---|---|
| The book | 86 |
| Page-by-page notes | 87-88 |
| Interactive Activities | 89-90 |
| Resource Sheets | 91-101 |

Introduction

# PREFACE

**Dealing with everyday challenges**

For many young people with the more severe forms of learning difficulty, catching a bus to school or going into a shop by themselves for the first time are major challenges, the end of months of preparation and planning. But once achieved, the student can be seen to have moved forward significantly, and to have new horizons.

Teachers will routinely be encouraging their students to tackle new social skills and life skills, both large and small, as part of their personal development and independence training. Hopefully this resource will provide them with the incentive to take on new targets and challenges and experience a real sense of achievement.

## HOW TO INSTALL THE CD-ROM

1. Insert the CD-ROM into the CD-ROM drive. After a few seconds an installation screen should appear. If the screen does not appear, double-click on the My Computer icon, double-click on the CD-ROM icon, and then on setup.exe to start the installation.

2. Click 'Next' to proceed through the installation screens. If you wish to change the installation point, click 'Change'.

3. Click 'Install" to begin the installation.

4. When the installation is complete, click 'Finish' to exit the installer.

5. Double-click the 'Everyday Challenges' icon on the desktop to start the program.

# ABOUT THESE RESOURCES

This pack is made up of a CD-ROM and a Teacher's Book of notes and photocopiable resource sheets. As a teaching resource for Entry Level 1-2 it complements the six titles in the *Everyday Challenges* series:

- *Travelling by Yourself*
- *Moving On to College*
- *Swimming a Length*
- *Learning to Speak Up*
- *Shopping for Mum*
- *Shopping for Clothes*

It includes many follow-up activities, and offers teachers two key teaching tools:

- The facility to give whiteboard lessons.
- The facility to make and save changes to the text, offering opportunities to make abridged or personalised versions for individual students.

## THE CD-ROM

As long as you have purchased the Activity Pack, no extra site licences are needed.

Instructions for installing the CD-ROM can be found on the opposite page.

The CD-ROM contains both the text and illustrations of the six titles listed above, as well as a number of other valuable features:

- Audio (optional).
- Editable text.
- 15 Interactive Activities with teaching objectives.
- All Resource Sheets are included in pdf format.

## THE TEACHER BOOK

This contains a commentary on the individual titles and an introduction to the series as a whole.

- Page-by-page teacher notes for each book.
- Explanations of the CD-ROM's basic functions.
- Notes on the Interactive Activities
- Hard copies of all photocopiable Resource Sheets (you may copy these freely).
- Ideas for discussion and further activities.

## THE READERS

The activities in this Pack are designed to work with and alongside these six reading books. They are available singly or in money-saving packs of 6.

Contact our distributor:
Phone: 01904 431213
Fax: 01904 430868
Email: orders@yps-publishing.co.uk

Or visit our website:
www.senpress.co.uk

**Travelling by Yourself**
Single copy:
978-1-905579-00-6
Value Pack (6 copies):
978-1-905579-10-5

**Moving On to College**
Single copy:
978-1-905579-36-5
Value Pack (6 copies):
978-1-905579-37-2

**Swimming a Length**
Single copy:
978-1-905579-26-6
Value Pack (6 copies):
978-1-905579-28-0

**Learning to Speak Up**
Single copy:
978-1-905579-40-2
Value Pack (6 copies):
978-1-905579-41-9

**Shopping for Mum**
Single copy:
978-1-905579-05-1
Value Pack (6 copies):
978-1-905579-15-0

**Shopping for Clothes**
Single copy:
978-1-905579-25-9
Value Pack (6 copies):
978-1-905579-27-3

Browse and buy at
www.senpress.co.uk

Read more about our other series:
Work Experience, Scary Things,
Simple Meals, Ups and Downs.

sen PRESS

Introduction

## THE INTERACTIVE ACTIVITIES

The topics of the Interactive Activities included on the CD-ROM are set out in the box below.

| BOOK TITLE | INTERACTIVE ACTIVITIES |
| --- | --- |
| *Introductory Activity** | What is a Challenge? |
| *Travelling by Yourself* | Crossing the Road<br>Bus Numbers and Destinations<br>What To Do If... |
| *Moving On to College* | Following Directions<br>Dinner Money<br>Using the Canteen |
| *Swimming a Length* | Swimming<br>Exercise and Healthy Living |
| *Learning to Speak Up* | Speaking Up<br>Making Decisions Together |
| *Shopping for Mum* | Choices in the Shops<br>Being Careful with Your Money |
| *Shopping for Clothes* | What's Your Size?<br>Tips for Clothes Shopping |
| *Closing Activity** | Ready for a Challenge? |

\* There is a generic two-part fifteenth activity which is not specific to any individual book, but which will be tackled in two halves. The first part, 'What is a Challenge?', should be used before reading the *Everyday Challenges* books (students will be asked to think about what 'challenge' means). The second part, 'Ready for a Challenge?', should be tackled at the very end (when students are asked to state how they would feel about tackling the different challenges mentioned in each book). There is more information about this activity after these prelims and before the 'Travelling By Yourself' section of this book.

# Introduction

## THE RESOURCE SHEETS

*You are free to copy these sheets freely for use in your school/college.*

There are nine resource sheets for each book:

## THE BOOK AND ACTIVITIES FEEDBACK SHEET
Students write a sentence or two giving their views on the book and activities they've just tackled and think about anything they might have learned.

## STUDENT RECORD SHEET
A record sheet for the teacher to record the various activities undertaken by the student in this part of the topic, and the level achieved.

## HOW WELL DID YOU READ?
Ten simple true or false questions related to the text.

## COVER SHEET
A sheet for students to decorate, and use as a cover for their resource sheets folder.

## WORDS AND PICTURES
Match ten words with illustrations from the book.

## PICTURE SEARCH
Search the book for six illustrations, then write a sentence about each of them.

## KEYWORD FLASHCARDS
Sixteen related words taken from the text. These need to be printed onto card and cut up.

## WORDSEARCH
Ten key words chosen from the flashcards.

## SPOT THE DIFFERENCE
An illustration from the book with six details changed.

---

*Travelling By Yourself* has two extra worksheets: 'My Independent Travel' and 'How Well Did Adam Do?'

The 'What is a Challenge?' / 'Ready for a Challenge?' Interactive Activity has a supporting worksheet entitled 'My Challenges'.

Introduction

## KEY TO BUTTONS AND ICONS IN THE INTERACTIVE ACTIVITIES

### GENERAL

| | |
|---|---|
| *[Book cover: Travelling by Yourself]* | Click on a book cover to read that story. |
| *[Interactive activities button]* | Takes you to a menu of all the activities on the CD-ROM. |
| *[Resource sheets button]* | Takes you to a menu of PDF worksheets and other resources. |
| *[Spanner/key icon]* | Takes you to the settings screen where you can turn audio on or off for the whole CD-ROM or activate a darker panel around the text to make it easier to read. |
| *[i icon]* | Information about this product. (NOTE: In some activities this button will bring up a word definition) |
| *[sen Press icon]* | Information about the publisher. |
| *[Quit button]* | Will exit the program. |
| *[Story button]* | This will take you out of an activity back to the story if that is how you got to the activity. |
| *[Menu button]* | This will take you out of an activity back to the activities menu if that is how you got to the activity. |
| *[Ear icon]* | Will play the audio again. (This button is only available when the audio is activated.) |
| *[Next button]* | Move on to the next screen. |
| *[Am I right? button]* | Click this to find out if your have completed an exercise correctly. |
| *[Play again button]* | Click this to repeat an exercise. The content will often change to provide some variety. |
| *[Help button]* | Will provide simple assistance if you get stuck or forget what to do. |

Closes a pop-up box or panel.

Tells you how far through the activity you are. Each spot represents a screen.

## STORY CONTROLS

**Start again** — Returns to the cover of the book.

**Next page** — Turns on a page.

**Previous page** — Turns back a page.

**Edit text** — Allows you to alter the text in the story.

**Clear text** — Deletes all text on the page so you can add your own.

**Restore text** — Reverts to the original text.

## SPECIAL TEACHER CONTROLS

Mutes the audio.

Turns muted audio back on.

(Stories only) Saves edited text. This allows you to create personalised versions. A system dialog box will open to allow you to save to your computer

## Introduction

(Stories only) Loads previously saved edited text. Find the version you want via the system dialog box that opens.

Skips forward a screen.

Skips back a screen.

**Teacher notes** Brings up teacher notes for an activity.

**Prompts** (Stories only) Reveals discussion points related to each page.

**NOTE** If any button appears black and has no icon, that function is not currently available.

# HOW TO USE THIS ACTIVITY PACK

The Activity Pack as a whole offers teachers the opportunity to focus, with their students, on challenges and the part they play in their personal development.

It is a flexible resource designed specially for Life Skills and Social Skills training and may be used in many ways.

### 1. For group activities

- *Whiteboard lessons* to introduce the main theme - 'challenges' - as well as the individual books and their activities
- *Follow-up reading* using the books themselves, the flashcards and interactive activities
- A *co-ordinated project for the group* – that covers reading, writing and IT work and that leads to students producing a portfolio of work. The resource sheets provided and print-outs from a number of the activities could be augmented with photographs of visits to clothes shops, supermarkets or swimming pools and personal writing
- As a *supporting, cross-curricular resource* to be used selectively for other modules being undertaken - eg personal development, healthy lifestyles, independence, money, personal safety, developing personal tastes
- As a *basis for discussion* on the achievements students would most value

### 2. For individual work

- Preparing for challenges similar to those in the books - eg independent travel, learning to swim, going to college
- For working out more relevant personal challenges or targets
- For additional literacy work

# READING AGES

| Title | Fry Readability Graph | Flesch-Kincaid Formula |
|---|---|---|
| *Travelling by Yourself* | 6.0 | 6.17 |
| *Moving On to College* | 6.0 | 5.93 |
| *Swimming a Length* | 6.25 | 6.08 |
| *Learning to Speak Up* | 6.0 | 6.15 |
| *Shopping for Mum* | 6.0 | 5.62 |
| *Shopping for Clothes* | 6.0 | 5.82 |

# GENERIC INTERACTIVE ACTIVITY

As well as Interactive Activites related directly to each book, the CD-ROM contains a two-part generic activity which is not specific to any individual book. It is designed to be tackled in two halves.

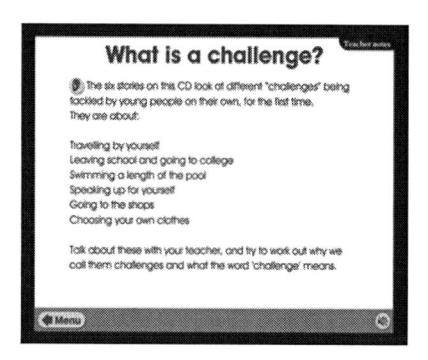

## PART 1: 'WHAT IS A CHALLENGE?' INTERACTIVE ACTIVITY

This first part should be used before reading the *Everyday Challenges* books. Students will be asked to think about what 'challenge' means.

### DEFINITION OF 'CHALLENGE'
*its different layers of meaning in this context*

- It's a test that we are likely to find difficult.
- It's something we'll have to tackle by ourselves.
- We'll probably be worried that we won't succeed.
- We'll need courage and determination.
- They offer us opportunities to develop as people and gain self-confidence.

**NB** be prepared for some students who confuse challenges of a personal development kind with aggressive challenges and dangerous 'dare' games they may have experienced.

### OBJECTIVES
Before tackling the activities, students think about the meaning of the word and...

- The challenges they face (or have faced) in their own lives.
- The challenges contained in the books.
- The importance of facing up to challenges.
- What it feels like to take on a challenge and succeed (and fail).
- Challenges that are real for some but not for others.
- Personal challenges that they might feel ready to set themselves.

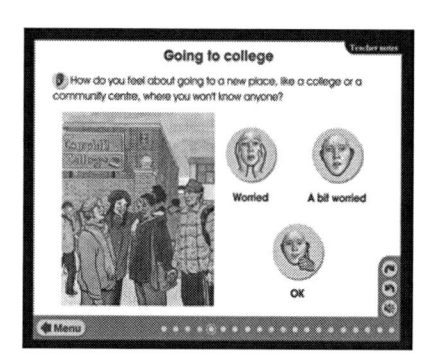

## PART 2: 'READY FOR A CHALLENGE?' INTERACTIVE ACTIVITY

This second part should be tackled after reading the *Everyday Challenges* books.

### OUTLINE
A questionnaire-type activity in which students consider how they might fare faced with the various challenges in the books. For a record of their answers, a print-out is available.

### FOLLOW-UP ACTIVITIES

- Discussion of these and other challenges that the students identify.
- Students identify goals/challenges for themselves – small or large – and plan how they might tackle these (with help).
- Various role-play opportunities.

# GENERIC WORKSHEET

The worksheet on the following page can be used in conjunction with this two-part Interactive Activity.

*xi*

# My challenges

Challenges aren't always big things.

Try to think of some of the things that you have done this year – things that you found difficult but you still did them by yourself. For example:

- Getting through medical treatment
- Speaking to someone for the first time
- Paying for something in a shop
- Doing something in school assembly

..............................................................................................

..............................................................................................

..............................................................................................

..............................................................................................

..............................................................................................

..............................................................................................

..............................................................................................

© SEN Press 2008. All rights reserved.

# FOR YOUR NOTES

# RESOURCES FOR 'TRAVELLING BY YOURSELF'

'TRAVELLING BY YOURSELF'

EVERYDAY CHALLENGES SERIES

LEVEL: 1-2

READING AGE: 6.0 YEARS

24 PAGES

545 WORDS

## KEY THEMES

Independent travel.

Journey planning.

Timekeeping.

Road safety.

Independence.

Concentration on the bus.

Self-confidence and self-esteem.

Talking to strangers.

## THE NARRATIVE

It's Adam's big day. He is going to school by bus, by himself, for the first time.

Everything goes well until he gets on the bus. Then a friendly woman he is sitting next to starts talking to him and showing him photographs of her grandchildren.

As a result, he nearly forgets his stop and nearly leaves his school bag behind.

Despite its narrative form, the book touches on all the main issues relating to young people travelling by themselves.

Resources for: 'Travelling by Yourself'

# PAGE BY PAGE NOTES FOR THE TEACHER

## TRAVELLING BY YOURSELF: PAGE 1

- Discuss feelings: Adam's and his mum's.
- Imagine a conversation between the two of them as Adam is leaving.
- Work out what Adam might be taking with him (bus pass, mobile phone, the school's telephone number, personal details on a card in case he gets lost etc).

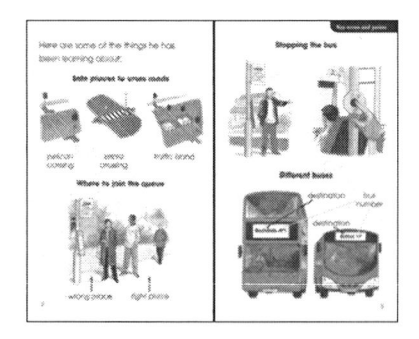

## TRAVELLING BY YOURSELF: PAGES 2-3

- Get the students to talk about the crossings and their differences.
- The pedestrian's point of view and the motorist's point of view.
- Check that students are familiar with the key terms used on these pages (pelican/zebra crossings, single/double decker buses etc).

## TRAVELLING BY YOURSELF: PAGES 4-5

- Study the details in the picture. What do they reveal about the sort of place Adam lives in? What are the clues? (eg aeroplane climbing - near an airport? The tall building - flats or offices?) This picture-building can continue as more is revealed on subsequent pages.

## TRAVELLING BY YOURSELF: PAGES 6-7

- Look for more clues relating to the place where Adam lives.
- The clock on the side of the office block – what time is it?
- The satellite dish – what's it for?
- Ask how *they* would get across the road to the bus stop?

# Resources for: 'Travelling by Yourself'

## TRAVELLING BY YOURSELF: PAGES 8-9

- Focus on pelican crossings and how they work.
- Does the green man appear straight away after pressing the button?
- What does a *flashing* green man signify?

## TRAVELLING BY YOURSELF: PAGES 10-11

- Look closely at each person in the queue and try to work out where each might be going at that time of the morning.
- Will they all be waiting for the same bus? (clue on the bus stop).
- Which ones might be going to work?
- Discuss queueing and what happens when people don't queue.

## TRAVELLING BY YOURSELF: PAGES 12-13

- Ask students if they know any local bus numbers and which routes the buses take. Do they use buses to get to town?
- Talk about the different colours, shapes and sizes of buses and the reasons for the differences.

## TRAVELLING BY YOURSELF: PAGES 14-15

- Talk about bus passes (if you know!): who is eligible for one, how to get one etc. Can you use them at holiday times?
- Do students know what a bus pass looks like? What information is on it?
- If you pay, does the driver give change?
- Is there a *best* place to sit? Upstairs or downstairs? Visibility?

## TRAVELLING BY YOURSELF: PAGES 16-17

- Talking to strangers: does stranger-danger still apply now students are older? Go through a number of different circumstances.
- When is it right to be suspicious of strangers?

# Resources for: 'Travelling by Yourself'

## TRAVELLING BY YOURSELF: PAGES 18-19

- Mention the dangers of distractions – chatting, watching and listening to other passengers, daydreaming – and not checking where the bus has got to.
- The importance of being able to see out of the window, especially when it's dark or raining and condensation makes visibility poor.

## TRAVELLING BY YOURSELF: PAGES 20-21

- Get students to suggest Adam's options if he missed his stop.
- The *What to Do If…* Interactive Activity (see page 7) looks at a number of situations to be prepared for.
- What happens to things that have been left on the bus by mistake?

## TRAVELLING BY YOURSELF: PAGES 22-23

- Evaluate Adam's performance.
- Should Adam have owned up to nearly missing his stop?

## TRAVELLING BY YOURSELF: PAGE 24

- Skip through the ten points but don't labour them too much. Concentrate on just a few points that you feel you may not have dealt with adequately in the preceding pages. Points 3, 4 and 5 are well covered in the activities *Crossing the Road* and *Bus Numbers and Destinations*. Point 10 is covered by the activity *What to Do If…*.

Resources for: 'Travelling by Yourself'

# INTERACTIVE ACTIVITIES

There are three interactive activities that develop key themes in the narrative. They are designed for use both on whiteboards and individual PCs.

## 1. 'CROSSING THE ROAD' INTERACTIVE ACTIVITY TEACHER NOTES

This activity examines in some detail different aspects of crossing the road and road safety. It contains a mixture of simple activities: true and false, drag and drop and a cloze passage.

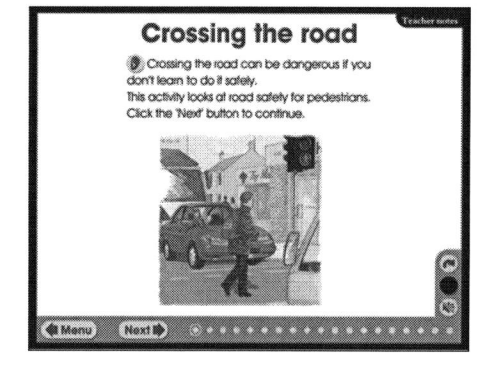

### RELATES TO: 'TRAVELLING BY YOURSELF' PAGES 2, 6, 7, 8, 9
### LEVEL: 1-2

#### OBJECTIVES

Students learn the essentials of road crossing:
- Safe and dangerous crossing points.
- How to cross the road.
- Seeing and being seen.
- Crossing roads in bad weather and in the dark.

#### FOLLOW-UP ACTIVITIES

- Discussion – students relate their own experiences of crossing roads, their feelings, the risks and dangers etc.
- Regular practice on trips into town.
- A study of the Green Cross Code.
- Independent travel training for suitable students.

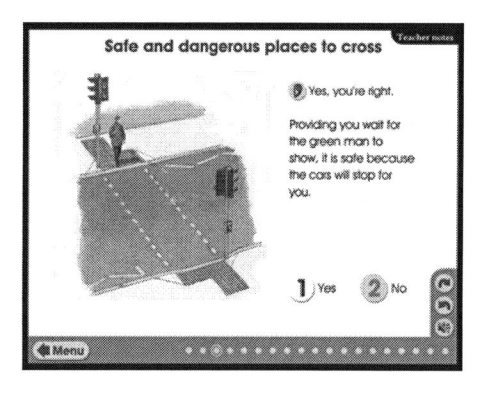

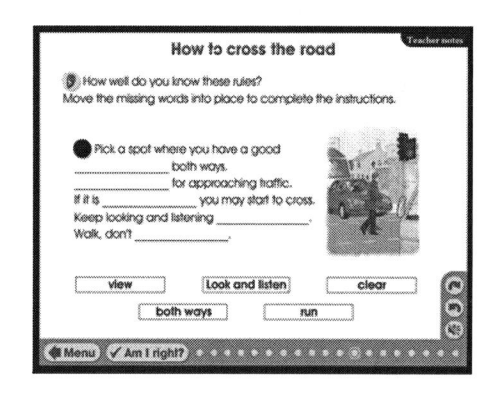

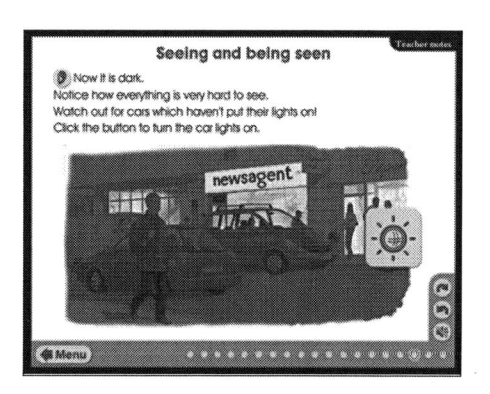

5

Resources for: 'Travelling by Yourself'

## 2. 'BUSES – NUMBERS AND DESTINATIONS' INTERACTIVE ACTIVITY TEACHER NOTES

This is a simple, bespoke activity which tests students' ability to distinguish *their* bus from other buses approaching the bus stop. Teachers can alter the bus's colour, destination, type (single or double decker) and number to make the activity relevant. The activity continues until students have correctly identified their bus *four times*.

### RELATES TO: 'TRAVELLING BY YOURSELF' PAGES 12-13
### LEVEL: 1-2

#### OBJECTIVES

- Students learn to identify buses by their numbers and destinations.
- Students learn to distinguish *their* bus from other buses.
- Students learn the names of towns or villages near them.
- Practical number and word recognition.

#### FOLLOW-UP ACTIVITIES

- A trip to the local bus station for students to experience the number of different routes and destinations that buses take.
- Look at the bus timetable for a familiar route and the information it gives, eg where the buses stop along the route and their frequency.
- Look at a local map and pick out the names of local places featured on the front of different buses.

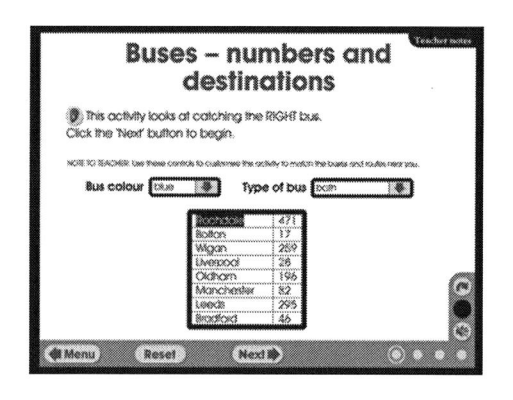

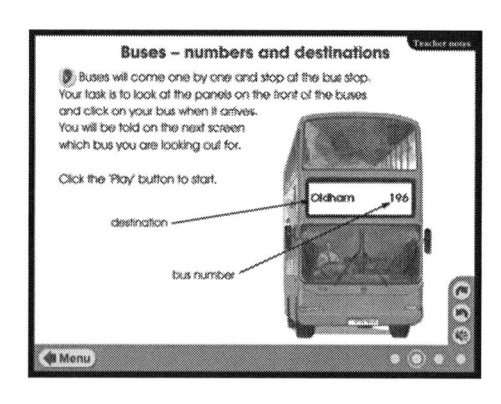

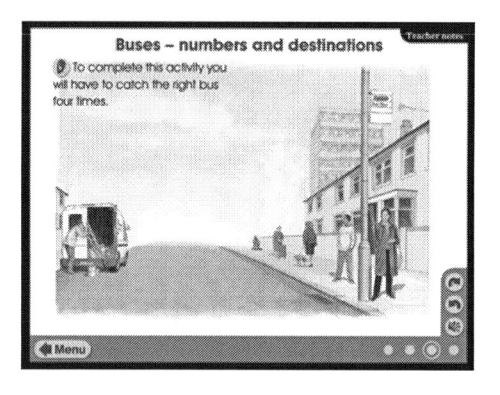

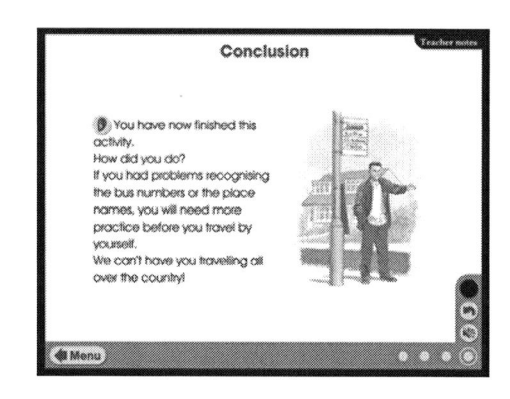

# 3. 'WHAT TO DO IF...' INTERACTIVE ACTIVITY TEACHER NOTES

This is a text-based multiple choice activity in which students are asked to consider the best course of action in a number of difficult travel situations.

**NB** it is best for this activity to be directed by the teacher as the situations need to be discussed. Before starting, it would be advisable for teachers to satisfy themselves that the advice given in the activity corresponds with what they teach their students to do.

## RELATES TO: 'TRAVELLING BY YOURSELF' PAGES 18-21
## LEVEL: 1-2

### OBJECTIVES

Students consider, through six 'worst-case scenarios':

- The best course of action to take in each.
- General procedures to follow when in difficulty.

### FOLLOW-UP ACTIVITIES

- Encourage students to talk about difficult situations they have found themselves in and what they did - eg arriving home and finding the front door locked and not having a key to get in.
- Think of more 'What To Do If...' situations.
- Various role-play situations emerging from the discussions above.

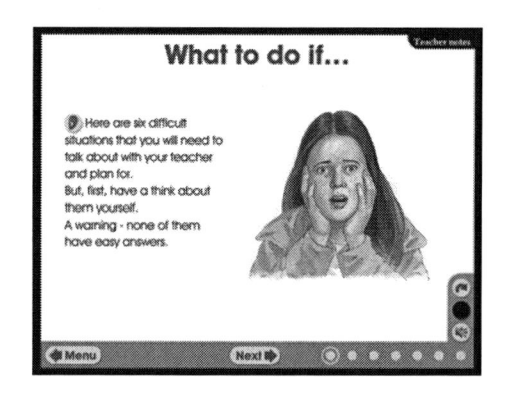

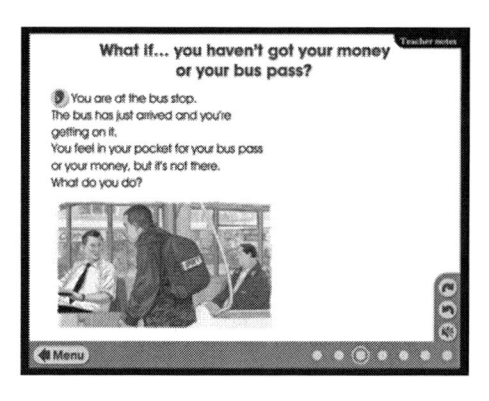

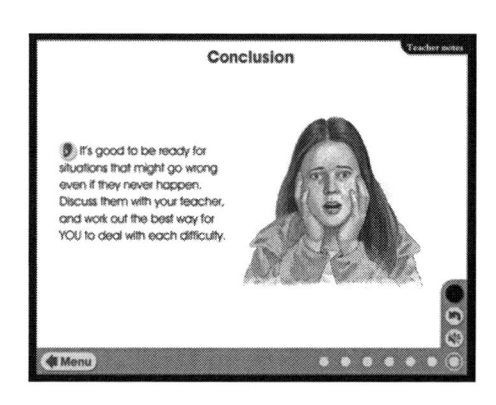

Resources for: 'Travelling by Yourself'

# RESOURCE SHEETS

**You may copy these sheets freely for use in your school/college.**

There are eleven resource sheets which relate specifically to *Travelling by Yourself*:

## THE BOOK AND ACTIVITIES FEEDBACK SHEET
Students write a sentence or two giving their views on the book and activities they've just tackled and think about anything they might have learned.

## STUDENT RECORD SHEET
A record sheet for the teacher to record the various activities undertaken by the student in this part of the topic, and the level achieved.

## HOW WELL DID YOU READ?
Ten simple true or false questions related to the text.

## COVER SHEET
A sheet for students to decorate, and use as a cover for their resource sheets folder.

## WORDS AND PICTURES
Match ten words with illustrations from the book.

## PICTURE SEARCH
Search the book for six illustrations, then write a sentence about each of them.

## KEYWORD FLASHCARDS
Sixteen travel-related words taken from the text. These need to be printed onto card and cut up.

## WORDSEARCH
Ten key words chosen from the flashcards.

## SPOT THE DIFFERENCE
An illustration from the book with six details changed.

## MY INDEPENDENT TRAVEL

Students answer quetiosn about their own travel arrangements: "My bus goes at...", "I will take these things with me..." etc.

## HOW WELL DID ADAM DO?
Students review how well Adam did on his journey - seven yes/no questions, marks out of ten - and write a sentence saying what he did wrong.

# The book and activities feedback sheet

1. Say what you thought of the book.
(Could you read it and understand it? Did you find it interesting? A bit? Was it boring? Did you like any of the illustrations? Which one(s)?)

..................................................................................................

..................................................................................................

..................................................................................................

2. Say what you thought of the interactive activities.
(Did you find them easy to use? Did you enjoy any of them? Which one(s)?)

..................................................................................................

..................................................................................................

..................................................................................................

3. Say if you learned anything from either.

..................................................................................................

..................................................................................................

..................................................................................................

© SEN Press 2008. All rights reserved.

Resources for: 'Travelling by Yourself'

# Student record sheet
## Travelling by Yourself

..................................................has,

- Read the text - with help/without help

- Made a contribution to the discussion - yes/no

- Completed the *How well did you read*? exercise - with help/without help
  Score:..................

- Tackled the 16 flashcards and achieved this score:.....................

- Completed these interactive activities
    - Crossing the road
    - Buses - numbers and destinations
    - What to do if...

- Completed these additional tasks or activities:
    - ................................................................................
    - ................................................................................

- Completed these other resource sheets:
    - Book and activities feedback sheet
    - How well did Adam do?
    - Wordsearch
    - Word puzzle
    - Spot the difference
    - Cover drawing

- Other related challenges undertaken and lessons learned:
    - ................................................................................
    - ................................................................................
    - ................................................................................

© SEN Press 2008. All rights reserved.

# How well did you read?

Five of these are TRUE, and five are FALSE

| | | |
|---|---|---|
| 1. | Adam's mum was nervous. | TRUE / FALSE |
| 2. | It took Adam five minutes to walk to the bus stop. | TRUE / FALSE |
| 3. | He crossed the road at a zebra crossing. | TRUE / FALSE |
| 4. | Destination means the place where the bus is going. | TRUE / FALSE |
| 5. | Two buses came at the same time. | TRUE / FALSE |
| 6. | He caught the 471. | TRUE / FALSE |
| 7. | He sat upstairs on the top deck. | TRUE / FALSE |
| 8. | A woman showed him photographs of her children. | TRUE / FALSE |
| 9. | He nearly missed his stop. | TRUE / FALSE |
| 10. | He left his bag on the bus. | TRUE / FALSE |

© SEN Press 2008. All rights reserved.

# Travelling by Yourself

Name _____

Class _____

Resources for: 'Travelling by Yourself'

# Words and pictures

- Match up the words with their pictures.
  Draw a line between each pair

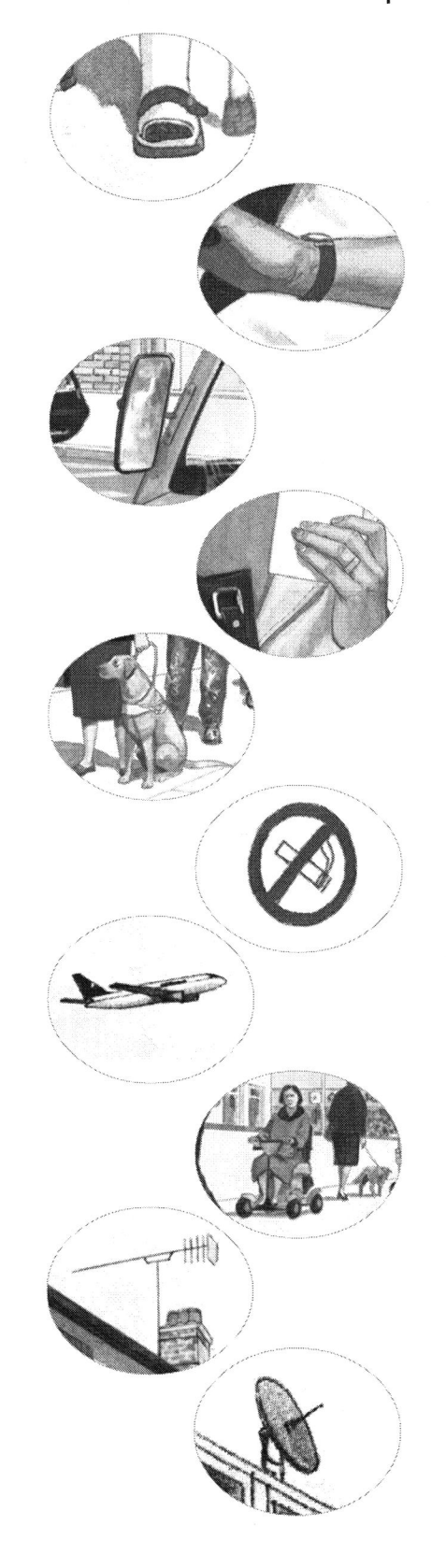

wing mirror

aeroplane

guide dog

plaster cast

wrist watch

satellite dish

television aerial

wedding ring

'no smoking' sign

invalid scooter

© SEN Press 2008. All rights reserved.

Resources for: 'Travelling by Yourself'

# Picture search

- Look for each of these illustrations.
- Write down which pages you found them on.
- Try putting each word into a sentence.

I found a **wing mirror** on page _____

*write your* wing mirror *sentence here*

I found a **guide dog** on page _____

*write your* guide dog *sentence here*

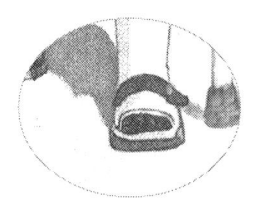

I found a **plaster cast** on page _____

*write your* plaster cast *sentence here*

I found an **aeroplane** on page _____

*write your* aeroplane *sentence here*

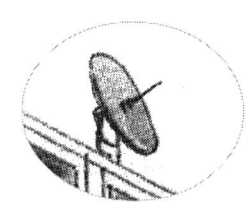

I found a **satellite dish** on page _____

*write your* satellite dish *sentence here*

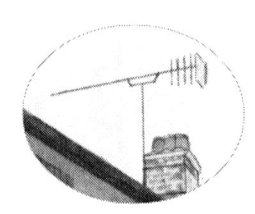

I found a **television aerial** on page _____

*write your* television aerial *sentence here*

© SEN Press 2008. All rights reserved.

# Key words flashcards

| | |
|---|---|
| queue | safe |
| pelican | zebra |
| traffic | destination |
| bus stop | button |

© SEN Press 2008. All rights reserved.

# Key words flashcards

| | |
|---|---|
| crossing | driver |
| single decker | double decker |
| bus pass | upstairs |
| downstairs | crowded |

# Wordsearch

Search for the hidden words from the lists in this grid.

| u | s | g | x | p | e | l | i | c | a | n | s |
|---|---|---|---|---|---|---|---|---|---|---|---|
| d | y | a | c | r | o | s | s | i | n | g | p |
| e | t | z | f | a | w | q | c | b | e | w | m |
| s | b | r | s | t | i | h | j | s | a | f | e |
| t | r | a | f | f | i | c | f | c | r | t | y |
| i | b | v | t | b | h | q | u | e | u | e | b |
| n | e | w | q | u | y | o | t | e | d | i | u |
| a | i | t | h | s | c | s | r | y | r | n | z |
| t | t | j | u | s | b | y | j | l | i | s | e |
| i | m | b | u | t | t | o | n | v | v | k | b |
| o | e | m | e | o | z | e | c | d | e | h | r |
| n | m | f | e | p | g | m | f | h | r | i | a |

queue  
safe  
pelican  
zebra  
traffic  

destination  
bus stop  
button  
crossing  
driver  

© SEN Press 2008. All rights reserved.

Resources for: 'Travelling by Yourself'

# Spot the difference

Can you spot the six differences in the pictures. Ring them on the picture on the right.

© SEN Press 2008. All rights reserved.

Resources for: 'Travelling by Yourself'

# My independent travel

(For students learning to travel independently)

1. I will leave the house at this time: ............
2. It will take me ........ minutes to get to the bus stop.
3. My bus leaves at this time: ..........
4. The number of my bus is: ..........
5. It will have this destination on the front: .....................
6. I will take these things with me:

................................................................................................
................................................................................................
................................................................................................
................................................................................................

7. When I am on the bus, I must remember to do these things:

................................................................................................
................................................................................................
................................................................................................
................................................................................................

8. In emergencies, this is what I will do:

................................................................................................
................................................................................................
................................................................................................
................................................................................................

© SEN Press 2008. All rights reserved.

Resources for: 'Travelling by Yourself'

# How well did Adam do?

Imagine you are following Adam on his journey to school...

1. Does he leave the house at the right time?           Yes/No

2. Does he cross the main road safely?                  Yes/No

3. Does he queue in the right place at the bus stop?    Yes/No

4. Does he get on the right bus?                        Yes/No

5. Has he remembered his bus pass?                      Yes/No

6. Does he behave well on the bus?                      Yes/No

7. Does he pay attention?                               Yes/No

Give him marks out of ten:                              /10

Tell him what he did wrong:

..............................................................................................

..............................................................................................

..............................................................................................

© SEN Press 2008. All rights reserved.

# RESOURCES FOR 'MOVING ON TO COLLEGE'

'MOVING ON TO COLLEGE'

EVERYDAY CHALLENGES SERIES

LEVEL: 1-2

READING AGE: 6.0 YEARS

16 PAGES

253 WORDS

## KEY THEMES

Leaving school and familiar surroundings.

Leaving friends behind.

Anxieties about change.

Adjusting to a larger, busier environment.

The canteen at lunchtime.

Different journey/changed routine.

Finding your way round.

Making new friends.

Growing up.

## THE NARRATIVE

Becky is 16. She and her Year 11 friends will be leaving school soon and she is getting anxious. She is going to college but her close friends aren't going with her. Her first impressions of the college don't make her feel any better and she almost convinces herself that she'll hate it.

The situations described in the book will allow students to talk about their worries, and will provide teachers with another opportunity to talk to their students about leaving school and the many challenges that lie ahead – no easy task!

# PAGE BY PAGE NOTES FOR THE TEACHER

### MOVING ON TO COLLEGE: PAGE 1

- Ask your students what they feel about leaving school at the end of the year. Do they know what their options are? Do they think that college is compulsory?

### MOVING ON TO COLLEGE: PAGES 2-3

- Leaving behind a small close-knit school community *will* be a major upheaval, and most students will obviously need to be talking about this all through the year so they are ready for it when it finally comes.
- Suggest reasons why they have to move on and the positives that they can look forward to as they become young adults.

### MOVING ON TO COLLEGE: PAGES 4-5

- Find out your students' feelings towards meeting their contemporaries in other schools. Are they suspicious? If so, what makes them feel this way? Do they think this feeling will last long?

### MOVING ON TO COLLEGE: PAGES 6-7

- Talk to the students about the nearest FE college and make comparisons with their school. Will they have been round it yet?...."

Resources for: 'Moving On to College'

## MOVING ON TO COLLEGE: PAGES 8-9

- Prepare students for college staff – and others – who may speak too fast and assume that they have been understood.

- Assure students that they are reading a story, and that they will be looked after better than Becky was.

## MOVING ON TO COLLEGE: PAGES 10-11

- The canteen: another potentially daunting experience that will require preparation. The two Interactive Activities 'Dinner Money' - see page 25 - and 'The Canteen' - see page 26 - examine many of the key issues.

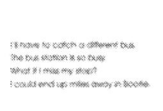

## MOVING ON TO COLLEGE: PAGES 12-13

- Consider the disruption to the students' daily routine if they will be travelling to college by themselves. How many students will this affect? How do they feel about catching a different bus and learning a new route? Does it worry them?

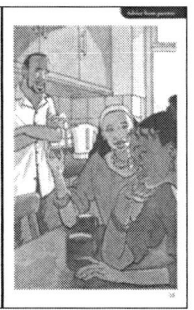

## MOVING ON TO COLLEGE: PAGES 14-15

- Introduce parents/step-parents/carers into the discussion. Has 'leaving school' been talked about at home? What was said?

- Do the students think that Becky's parents understand her feelings? Are they being helpful?

## MOVING ON TO COLLEGE: PAGE 16

- Talk about what might have made Becky change her mind about college.

Resources for: 'Moving On to College'

# INTERACTIVE ACTIVITIES

There are three interactive activities that develop key themes in the narrative. They are designed for use both on whiteboards and individual PCs.

## 1. 'FOLLOWING DIRECTIONS' INTERACTIVE ACTIVITY TEACHER NOTES

This is a multiple-choice activity in which students must listen and follow directions to a number of different places within a large building. It starts simply but gets progressively more difficult. It is designed to test the students' memory and concentration.

### RELATES TO: 'MOVING ON TO COLLEGE' PAGES 8-9

### LEVEL: 1-3

### OBJECTIVES

Students learn:
- The main terms – left/right, up/down etc – in direction giving.
- To listen very carefully to what they're told and retain the information in their heads.

### FOLLOW-UP ACTIVITIES

- Set students direction-finding tasks in the familiar surroundings of their school/college.
- Set students direction-finding tasks in less familiar surroundings, but follow them to make sure they don't get lost!
- Give students practice in *asking* for directions, stating clearly where they want to get to and asking for the directions to be repeated if necessary.

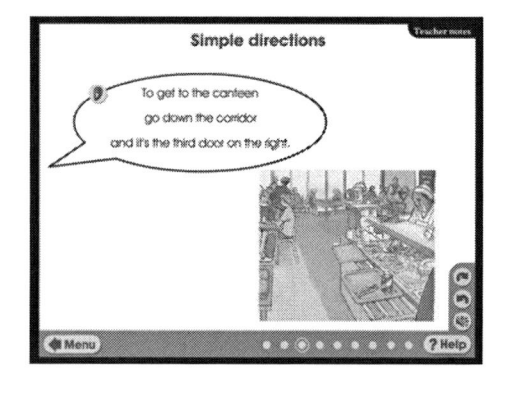

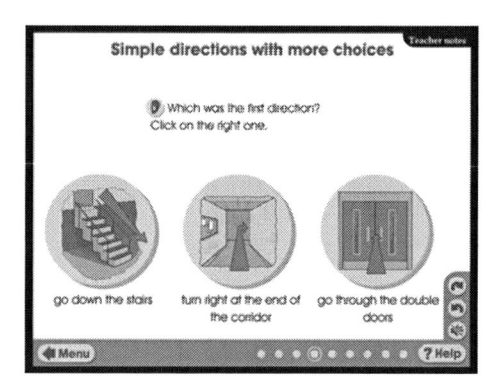

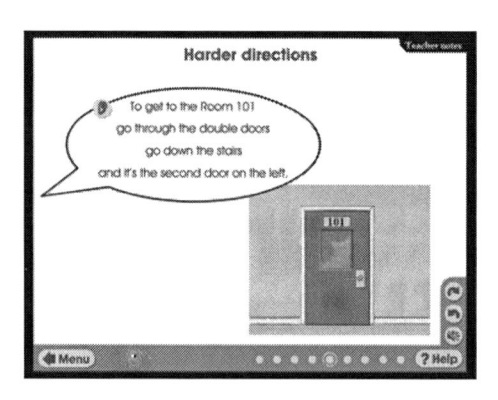

## 2. 'DINNER MONEY' INTERACTIVE ACTIVITY TEACHER NOTES

This is both a drag-and-drop and a multiple-choice activity. It involves coin recognition and the addition of two, then three coins, in preparation for the next Interactive Activity ('The Canteen' - see page 26 - that deals with choosing and paying for a meal in a canteen/café.

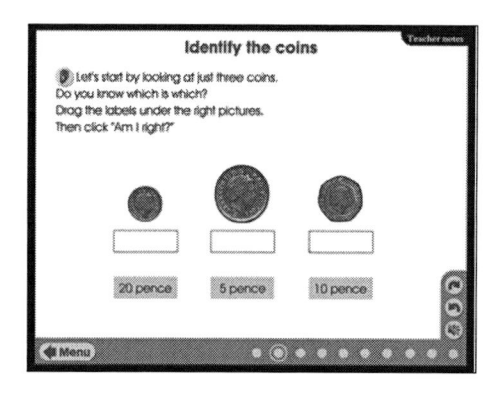

### RELATES TO: 'MOVING ON TO COLLEGE' PAGES 10-11

### LEVEL: 1-3

### OBJECTIVES

Students gain practice in:
- Identifying familiar everyday coins.
- The addition of two and three coins at a time.
- Ordering coins according to their value.

### FOLLOW-UP ACTIVITIES

- Reinforcement of these money handling exercises using *real* coins.
- Prepare for a trip to a café in town with clear tasks and objectives.

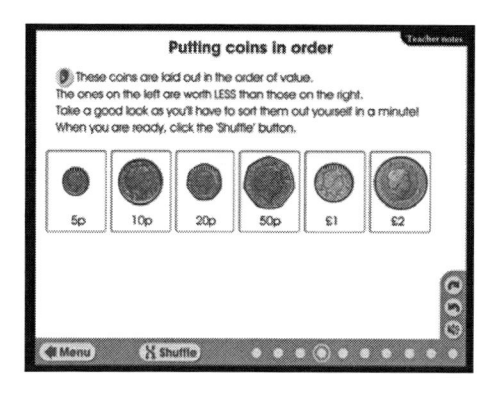

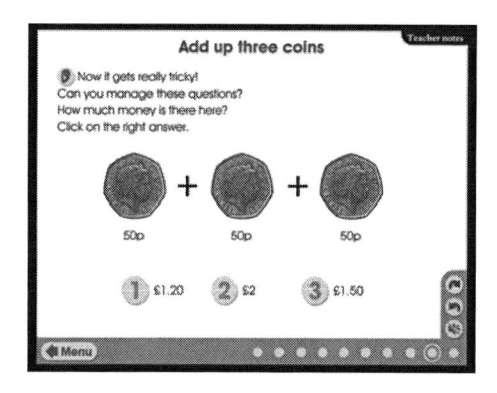

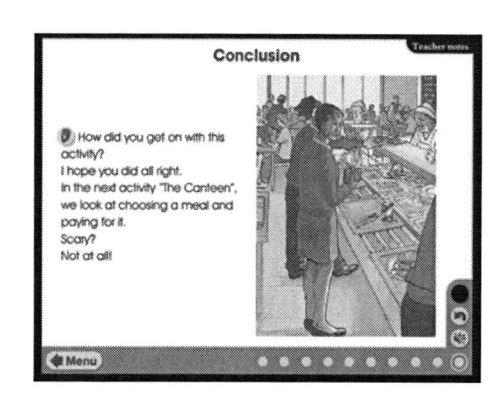

# 3. 'THE CANTEEN' INTERACTIVE ACTIVITY TEACHER NOTES

This is a bespoke activity that simulates a real-life canteen situation: students practise choosing their meal from the menu trying to keep to three different budgets - £5, £4 and £3.

## RELATES TO: 'MOVING ON TO COLLEGE' PAGES 10-11

## LEVEL: 1-3

### OBJECTIVES

Students gain valuable experience in:
- Examining and understanding a menu and its layout.
- Making choices from different sections of the menu.
- Learning the vocabulary of a standard canteen menu.
- Estimating the cost of their meal.
- Working to a budget.
- Returning an item if they have overspent.

### FOLLOW-UP ACTIVITIES

- Students design their own menu introducing new items.
- Word recognition (menu items) using flashcards - see pages 34-35.
- Use visits to a café or canteen to reinforce what they have prepared for.
- Role-play: students further practise different aspects of the two activities.

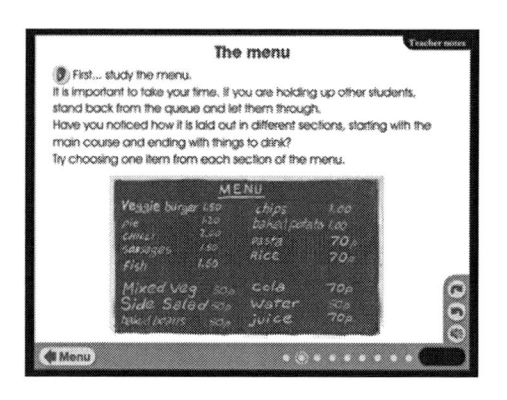

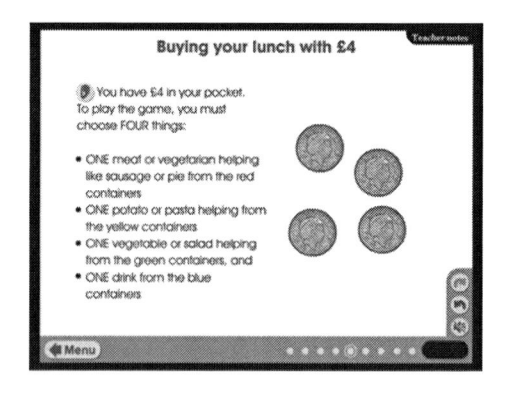

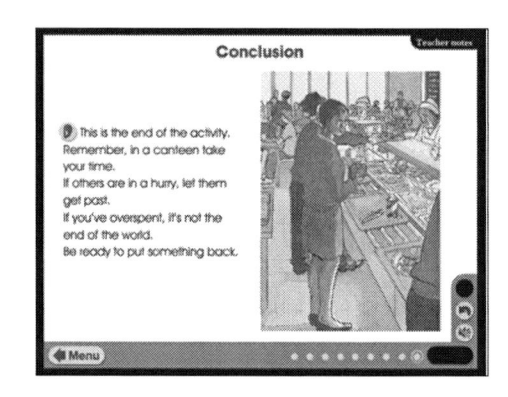

# RESOURCE SHEETS

**You may copy these sheets freely for use in your school/college.**

There are nine resource sheets which relate specifically to *Moving On to College:*

### THE BOOK AND ACTIVITIES FEEDBACK SHEET
Students write a sentence or two giving their views on the book and activities they've just tackled and think about anything they might have learned.

### STUDENT RECORD SHEET
A record sheet for the teacher to record the various activities undertaken by the student in this part of the topic, and the level achieved.

### HOW WELL DID YOU READ?
Ten simple true or false questions related to the text.

### COVER SHEET
A sheet for students to decorate, and use as a cover for their resource sheets folder.

### WORDS AND PICTURES
Match ten words with illustrations from the book.

### PICTURE SEARCH
Search the book for six illustrations, then write a sentence about each of them.

### KEYWORD FLASHCARDS
Sixteen college-related words taken from the text. These need to be printed onto card and cut up.

### WORDSEARCH
Ten key words chosen from the flashcards.

### SPOT THE DIFFERENCE
An illustration from the book with six details changed.

# The book and activities feedback sheet

1. Say what you thought of the book.

(Could you read it and understand it? Did you find it interesting? A bit? Was it boring? Did you like any of the illustrations? Which one(s)?)

..................................................................................................................

..................................................................................................................

..................................................................................................................

2. Say what you thought of the interactive activities.

(Did you find them easy to use? Did you enjoy any of them? Which one(s)?)

..................................................................................................................

..................................................................................................................

..................................................................................................................

3. Say if you learned anything from either.

..................................................................................................................

..................................................................................................................

..................................................................................................................

..................................................................................................................

© SEN Press 2008. All rights reserved.

Resources for: 'Moving On to College'

# Student record sheet
## Moving On to College

..................................................has,

- Read the text - with help/without help

- Made a contribution to the discussion - yes/no

- Completed the *How well did you read?* exercise - with help/without help
  Score:..................

- Tackled the 16 flashcards and achieved this score:.....................

- Completed these interactive activities
    - Following directions
    - Dinner money
    - The canteen

- Completed these additional tasks or activities:
    - ........................................................................................
    - ........................................................................................
    - ........................................................................................

- Completed these other resource sheets:
    - Book and activities feedback sheet
    - Wordsearch
    - Word puzzle
    - Spot the difference
    - Cover drawing

- Other related challenges undertaken and lessons learned:
    - ........................................................................................
    - ........................................................................................
    - ........................................................................................

© SEN Press 2008. All rights reserved.

# How well did you read?

Five of these are TRUE, and five are FALSE

| | | |
|---|---|---|
| 1. | Becky is sixteen. | TRUE / FALSE |
| 2. | She's in Year 10. | TRUE / FALSE |
| 3. | Her school uniform is green. | TRUE / FALSE |
| 4. | Her friends are going with her to college. | TRUE / FALSE |
| 5. | She got lost looking for the canteen. | TRUE / FALSE |
| 6. | She couldn't find the toilets. | TRUE / FALSE |
| 7. | She went to college by bus. | TRUE / FALSE |
| 8. | The college was called Camphall College. | TRUE / FALSE |
| 9. | Her parents said she would make new friends. | TRUE / FALSE |
| 10. | She hated her first term at college. | TRUE / FALSE |

© SEN Press 2008. All rights reserved.

# Moving On to College

Name _____

Class _____

© SEN Press 2008. All rights reserved.

# Words and pictures

- Match up the words with their pictures.
  Draw a line between each pair

fire exit sign

church spire

clipboard

bangle

knife and fork

menu

drain cover

goal post

drain pipe

school logo

© SEN Press 2008. All rights reserved.

# Picture search

- Look for each of these illustrations.
- Write down which pages you found them on.
- Try putting each word into a sentence.

I found a **fire exit sign** on page _____

*write your* fire exit *sentence here*

I found a **church spire** on page _____

*write your* church spire *sentence here*

I found a **clipboard** on page _____

*write your* clipboard *sentence here*

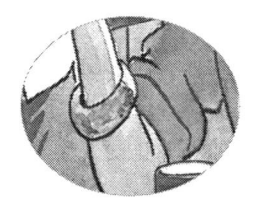

I found a **bangle** on page _____

*write your* bangle *sentence here*

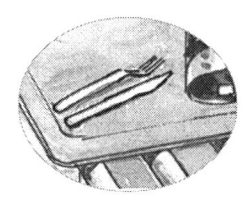

I found a **knife and fork** on page _____

*write your* knife and fork *sentence here*

I found a **menu** on page _____

*write your* menu *sentence here*

© SEN Press 2008. All rights reserved.

# Key words flashcards

| | |
|---|---|
| leaving | friend |
| college | toilet |
| stairs | floor |
| canteen | lunch |

# Key words flashcards

| | |
|---|---|
| choose | money |
| menu | turn left/right |
| soup<br>burger<br>pie | sausages<br>pizza<br>fish |
| chips<br>potato<br>baked beans | pasta<br>salad<br>chilli |

© SEN Press 2008. All rights reserved.

# Wordsearch

Search for the hidden words from the lists in this grid.

| r | t | b | m | c | h | o | o | s | e | h | a |
|---|---|---|---|---|---|---|---|---|---|---|---|
| l | e | a | v | i | n | g | h | n | p | a | f |
| h | b | c | t | e | e | u | y | s | l | r | r |
| y | t | d | g | c | a | n | t | e | e | n | i |
| f | g | t | m | y | l | m | o | t | f | n | e |
| k | y | c | o | l | l | e | g | e | q | u | n |
| a | e | i | n | o | u | j | f | r | v | b | d |
| a | f | y | e | m | n | i | s | s | v | c | p |
| o | l | z | y | h | n | l | u | n | c | h | l |
| t | o | i | l | e | t | h | y | v | o | e | j |
| y | o | v | e | a | h | e | j | m | n | p | a |
| r | r | q | c | s | t | a | i | r | s | v | a |

leaving  
friend  
college  
toilet  
stairs  

floor  
canteen  
lunch  
choose  
money  

© SEN Press 2008. All rights reserved.

# Spot the difference

Can you spot the six differences in the pictures. Ring them on the picture on the right.

# RESOURCES FOR 'SWIMMING A LENGTH'

**'SWIMMING A LENGTH'**

**EVERYDAY CHALLENGES SERIES**

**LEVEL: 1-2**

**READING AGE: 6.2 YEARS**

**16 PAGES**

**335 WORDS**

## KEY THEMES

The challenge of swimming.

Concerns and anxieties.

The comfort zone of the shallow end and the next step - venturing into deeper water.

Respect for the concerns of non-swimmers.

Peer-group support.

The courage needed to attempt a length for the first time.

Discovering self-confidence through achievement.

## THE NARRATIVE

It's Darren's big day. He is going to try to swim a length for the first time. He can do several widths but is reluctant to move out of the shallow end where he feels comfortable. Mr Woods, his teacher, urges him to tackle this larger challenge even though Darren is wary.

The book focuses on Darren and his reservations about swimming. For him, the challenge is not only to swim a length for the first time, but also to overcome these reservations. Its main objective is to address the concerns of those who haven't yet found confidence and enjoyment in swimming.

# PAGE BY PAGE NOTES FOR THE TEACHER

### SWIMMING A LENGTH: PAGE 1

- Introduce the theme of the book – swimming – and Darren who doesn't much like it.
- Ask who can swim a length/who hasn't yet swum a length; who likes/dislikes swimming and the reasons why.

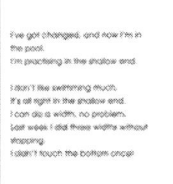

### SWIMMING A LENGTH: PAGES 2-3

- Ask the good swimmers to remember how old they were when they first swam a length and where it was. Was it a big challenge? How did they feel before *and* after?
- Are there any students in the group who are about to tackle a length for the first time? How do they view this prospect?

### SWIMMING A LENGTH: PAGES 4-5

- Look at these four common dislikes about swimming: who feels the same way? Are there any other concerns?
- Ask which of the four Darren dislikes the most.

### SWIMMING A LENGTH: PAGES 6-7

- What tells us that Darren isn't wanting to do it?
- What stops him from making an excuse?

(Neither answer is clearly stated: both require inference)

## Resources for: 'Swimming a Length'

### SWIMMING A LENGTH: PAGES 8-9

- Which end of the pool has Darren started from? Why is this?
- What advice would good swimmers in the group give to Darren as he sets off on his length?

### SWIMMING A LENGTH: PAGES 10-11

- Ask students to explain what has happened, and why swallowing water will affect Darren's swimming.
- Why is Mr Jones telling him to relax? What is Darren doing wrong?

### SWIMMING A LENGTH: PAGES 12-13

- What is Darren's worry?
- Which one in the picture is Susie? What is she doing wrong?

### SWIMMING A LENGTH: PAGES 14-15

- In a few seconds, Mr Jones will tell the other students to do something. What will he say?
- The other students are calling out "Come on, Darren!" Does this help him?

### SWIMMING A LENGTH: PAGE 16

- Talk together about Darren's achievement and how he will be feeling now.
- Talk about confidence and the difference it makes to all of us.
- Also give thought to the way our negative attitudes change when we have succeeded in something.

# INTERACTIVE ACTIVITIES

There are two Interactive Activities that develop key themes in the narrative. They are designed for use both on whiteboards and individual PCs.

## 1. 'SWIMMING' INTERACTIVE ACTIVITY TEACHER NOTES

This activity is a questionnaire, in which students consider their feelings towards different aspects of swimming. A print-out of their answers is available for their folders.

### RELATES TO: 'SWIMMING A LENGTH' PAGES 1-16

### LEVEL: 1-2

### OBJECTIVES

Students:

- Examine their own feelings towards swimming.
- Better appreciate the feelings of others who have difficulties swimming.

### FURTHER POINTS TO DISCUSS

- Darren's achievement and the qualities needed to swim his first length.
- Darren's 'comfort zone' (the shallow end of the pool).
- Other 'comfort zones' we all share.
- The importance of breaking with these if we are going to move forwards and develop as human beings.
- If Darren's achievement might change his attitude to swimming.

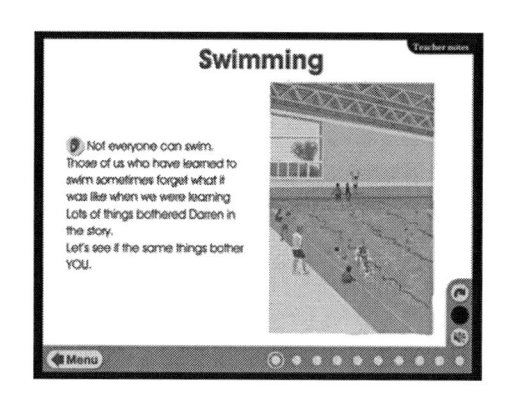

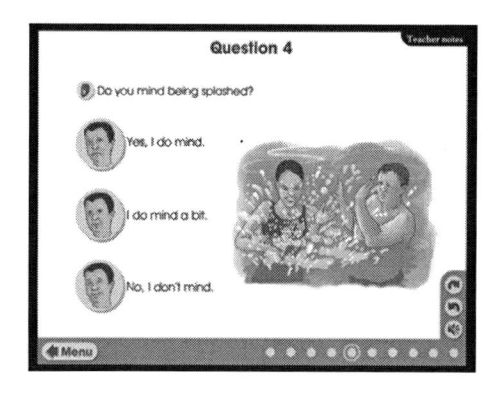

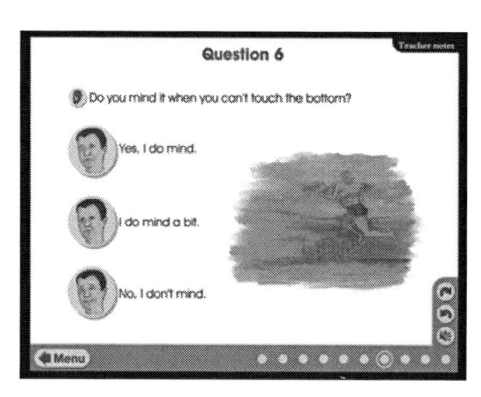

Resources for: 'Swimming a Length'

# 2. 'EXERCISE AND HEALTHY LIVING' INTERACTIVE ACTIVITY TEACHER NOTES

This is a simple multiple-choice activity, not specifically linked to *Swimming a Length*, which reminds students of healthy and unhealthy lifestyle choices.

## LEVEL: 1-2

### OBJECTIVES

Students learn to appreciate:
- Which foods are healthy, which are unhealthy, and why.
- That they should be starting to take responsibility for their own long-term health.
- The importance of a balanced diet.
- The need for regular exercise.

### FURTHER ACTIVITIES

- Discuss healthy and unhealthy lifestyles and what they mean in terms of everyday living.
- Look again at what makes some foods healthy and others unhealthy.
- Remind students of the down-side of packaged food e.g. extra salt, MSG, types of fat and artificial colouring, flavours and preservatives.
- Use trips to the shops to examine the information given on food packaging.
- Get students to record in a weekly diary what they have eaten, and the exercise they have taken.

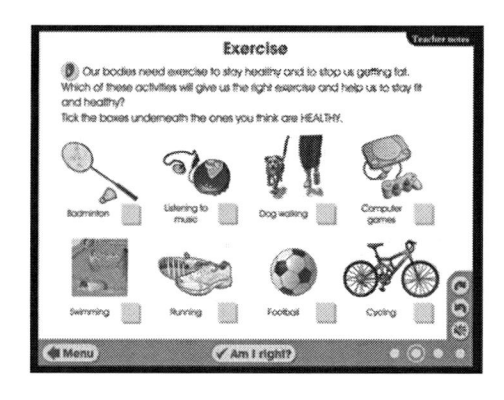

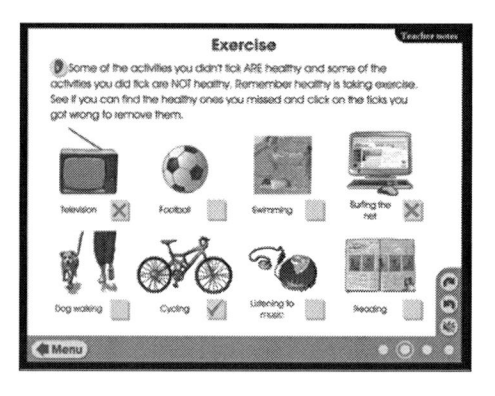

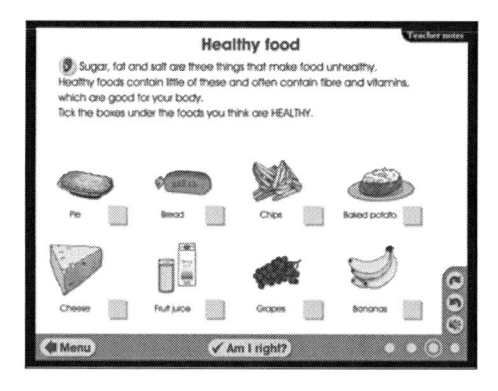

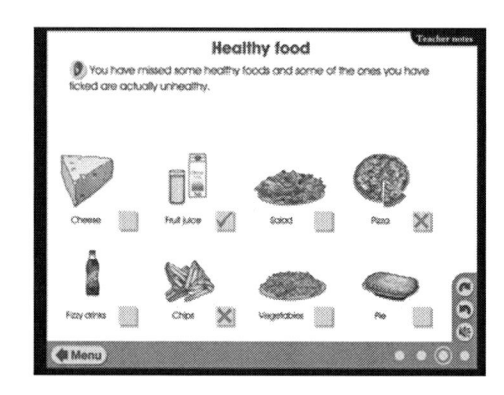

# RESOURCE SHEETS

**You may copy these sheets freely for use in your school/college.**

There are nine resource sheets which relate specifically to *Swimming a Length*:

### THE BOOK AND ACTIVITIES FEEDBACK SHEET
Students write a sentence or two giving their views on the book and activities they've just tackled and think about anything they might have learned.

### STUDENT RECORD SHEET
A record sheet for the teacher to record the various activities undertaken by the student in this part of the topic, and the level achieved.

### HOW WELL DID YOU READ?
Ten simple true or false questions related to the text.

### COVER SHEET
A sheet for students to decorate, and use as a cover for their resource sheets folder.

### WORDS AND PICTURES
Match ten words with illustrations from the book.

### PICTURE SEARCH
Search the book for six illustrations, then write a sentence about each of them.

### KEYWORD FLASHCARDS
Sixteen swimming-related words taken from the text. These need to be printed onto card and cut up.

### WORDSEARCH
Ten key words chosen from the flashcards.

### SPOT THE DIFFERENCE
An illustration from the book with six details changed.

Resources for: 'Swimming a Length'

# The book and activities feedback sheet

1. Say what you thought of the book.
(Could you read it and understand it? Did you find it interesting? A bit? Was it boring? Did you like any of the illustrations? Which one(s)?)

........................................................................................................

........................................................................................................

........................................................................................................

2. Say what you thought of the interactive activities.
(Did you find them easy to use? Did you enjoy any of them? Which one(s)?)

........................................................................................................

........................................................................................................

........................................................................................................

3. Say if you learned anything from either.

........................................................................................................

........................................................................................................

........................................................................................................

........................................................................................................

© SEN Press 2008. All rights reserved.

# Student record sheet
## Swimming a Length

....................................................has,

- Read the text - with help/without help

- Made a contribution to the discussion - yes/no

- Completed the *How well did you read?* exercise - with help/without help
  Score:..................

- Tackled the 16 flashcards and achieved this score:.....................

- Completed these interactive activities
    - Swimming
    - Exercise and healthy living

- Completed these additional tasks or activities:
    - ......................................................................................
    - ......................................................................................
    - ......................................................................................

- Completed these other resource sheets:
    - Book and activities feedback sheet
    - Wordsearch
    - Word puzzle
    - Spot the difference
    - Cover drawing

- Other related challenges undertaken and lessons learned:
    - ......................................................................................
    - ......................................................................................
    - ......................................................................................

© SEN Press 2008. All rights reserved.

# How well did you read?

Five of these are TRUE, and five are FALSE

1. Darren's teacher is called Mr Woods.　　TRUE / FALSE

2. He goes swimming every Monday.　　TRUE / FALSE

3. He has swum two widths of the pool without stopping.　　TRUE / FALSE

4. He is going to try swimming a length.　　TRUE / FALSE

5. He doesn't feel confident in deep water.　　TRUE / FALSE

6. He told Mr Woods he didn't feel well.　　TRUE / FALSE

7. He started his length at the deep end.　　TRUE / FALSE

8. Susie bumped into him.　　TRUE / FALSE

9. He was sick when he finished his length.　　TRUE / FALSE

10. The other students cheered him on.　　TRUE / FALSE

© SEN Press 2008. All rights reserved.

# Swimming a Length

Name _____

Class _____

# Words and pictures

- Match up the words with their pictures.
  Draw a line between each pair

information board

swimming floats

clothes lockers

foot baths

showers

towel

swimming cap

public gallery

steel roof beam

bench

Resources for: 'Swimming a Length'

# Picture search

- Look for each of these illustrations.
- Write down which pages you found them on.
- Try putting each word into a sentence.

I found a **swimming cap** on page _____

*write your* swimming cap *sentence here*

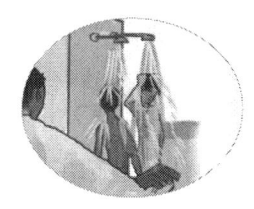

I found the **showers** on page _____

*write your* showers *sentence here*

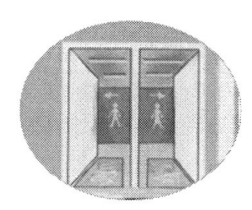

I found the **foot baths** on page _____

*write your* foot baths *sentence here*

I found a **steel roof beam** on page _____

*write your* steel roof beam *sentence here*

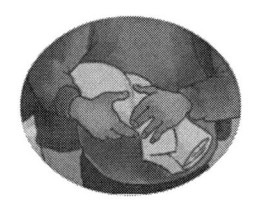

I found the **towel** on page _____

*write your* towel *sentence here*

I found a **bench** on page _____

*write your* bench *sentence here*

© SEN Press 2008. All rights reserved.

49

## Key words flashcards

| | |
|---|---|
| get changed | practise |
| strokes | kick |
| water | shower |
| splashing | cold |

# Key words flashcards

| | |
|---|---|
| sink | pool |
| width length | swimming baths |
| shallow end deep end | tired |
| ache | relax |

© SEN Press 2008. All rights reserved.

# Wordsearch

Search for the hidden words from the lists in this grid.

| k | s | p | l | a | s | h | i | n | g | b | a |
|---|---|---|---|---|---|---|---|---|---|---|---|
| r | s | o | y | j | c | v | d | m | u | b | o |
| m | i | o | f | s | y | h | k | o | j | p | e |
| d | t | l | s | t | r | o | k | e | s | w | v |
| s | i | n | k | o | p | v | i | b | m | i | p |
| o | o | f | d | w | y | b | c | i | c | o | r |
| w | a | t | e | r | c | p | k | g | o | z | a |
| u | s | t | b | m | n | r | f | h | l | n | c |
| r | c | q | u | o | t | f | y | i | d | o | t |
| s | h | o | w | e | r | t | q | n | u | o | i |
| e | o | m | e | h | i | b | p | v | u | j | s |
| g | e | t | c | h | a | n | g | e | d | b | e |

get changed      shower
practise         splashing
strokes          cold
kick             sink
water            pool

Resources for: 'Swimming a Length'

# Spot the difference

Can you spot the six differences in the pictures. Ring them on the picture on the right.

# RESOURCES FOR 'LEARNING TO SPEAK UP'

'LEARNING TO SPEAK UP'

EVERYDAY CHALLENGES SERIES

LEVEL: 1-2

READING AGE: 6.1 YEARS

16 PAGES

388 WORDS

## KEY THEMES

Making your personal likes, dislikes and preferences known.

Being quick off the mark when decisions are being made.

Whingeing.

Achieving the right level of assertiveness.

Give-and-take in family life.

The importance of developing personal tastes.

Having the courage to experiment.

Wanting more independence and seizing opportunities.

## THE NARRATIVE

Chris's mum, dad and sister seem to take all the decisions at home. He never gets to choose what he wants. That's because, when he is asked, he's too slow or reluctant to say what he wants and the opportunity slips by. His response is always to whinge rather than speak up at the time, until he finally seizes his chance when he's left on his own at the hairdresser's.

The book touches on many issues, but is essentially a short story for reading.

# PAGE BY PAGE NOTES FOR THE TEACHER

## LEARNING TO SPEAK UP: PAGE 1

- Build up a picture of Chris - how old he is, what he likes doing etc – and his family as you get further into the book.
- What does Chris tell us about himself on this first page?

## LEARNING TO SPEAK UP: PAGES 2-3

**NB** Some students may need help linking Chris's failure to speak up with him never getting his own way, on this and subsequent pages.

- Is Chris asked what he wants? Does he say? Is he happy with what he gets? What does he really want?

## LEARNING TO SPEAK UP: PAGES 4-5

- Once again: what does Chris really want? Does he say it?
- Maybe Chris needs to be a bit quicker off the mark and not miss his opportunity? What does he need to do?

## LEARNING TO SPEAK UP: PAGES 6-7

- Look at the shoes your group are wearing. Which students chose their own? Was there any discussion? Any disagreement? Who chose the shoes of the other students? Would they prefer different kinds of shoes? Are they *ready* to choose for themselves? What needs to happen?

Resources for: 'Learning to Speak Up'

## LEARNING TO SPEAK UP: PAGES 8-9

- Talk about different tastes in music – what most appeals to your students? Do they have CD collections? Do they have an i-pod? How, when and where do they listen to music? Are there arguments?

## LEARNING TO SPEAK UP: PAGES 10-11

- Talk to students about being 16 or thereabouts: growing up, developing as young people, wanting more independence. How do they demonstrate that they're ready for it?
- Is Chris's mum wrong to go into the hairdresser's with him?

## LEARNING TO SPEAK UP: PAGES 12-13

- Talk about going to the hairdresser's. Does everyone go? Where? Accompanied or unaccompanied? Who chooses? What do they ask for? Do they have the same every time?

## LEARNING TO SPEAK UP: PAGES 14-15

- Talk about hairstyles: those of film stars and celebrities, stylish ones that other young people have, how they feel about changing and experimenting.

## LEARNING TO SPEAK UP: PAGE 16

- Talk about what Chris has done: how he feels now (and might feel later on); the likely consequences when his mum returns; if he has done anything wrong or foolish etc.

# INTERACTIVE ACTIVITIES

There are two Interactive Activities that develop key themes in the narrative. They are designed for use both on whiteboards and individual PCs.

## 1. 'SPEAKING UP' INTERACTIVE ACTIVITY TEACHER NOTES

This is a bespoke activity involving dialogue between Chris and his family in a series of speech bubbles, with audio. As well as the weak answers that Chris gives in the book, there is the opportunity for him to say what he really wants, and students are shown how this can alter the outcome.

### RELATES TO: 'LEARNING TO SPEAK UP' PAGES 1-16

### LEVEL: 1-2

### OBJECTIVES

Students learn:

- How they can influence decisions by making their views known.
- How compromises are necessary and achievable.
- How *some* assertiveness is a good thing as long as they don't demand their own way every time.
- That whingeing won't get them anywhere.

### FOLLOW-UP ACTIVITIES

- Help students, unused to speaking up for themselves, to think up an appropriate place to start being more assertive.
- Talk about experimenting with different styles of clothes or haircuts.
- Discuss with students situations in which they feel ignored.
- Role-play situations from the book.

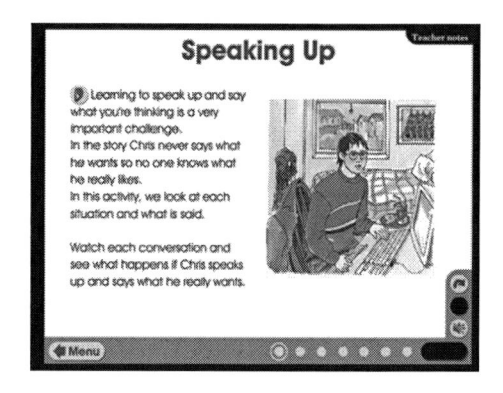

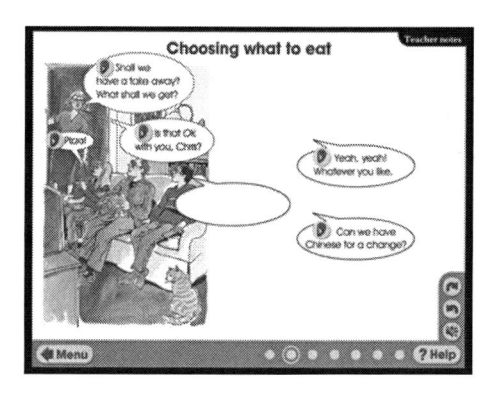

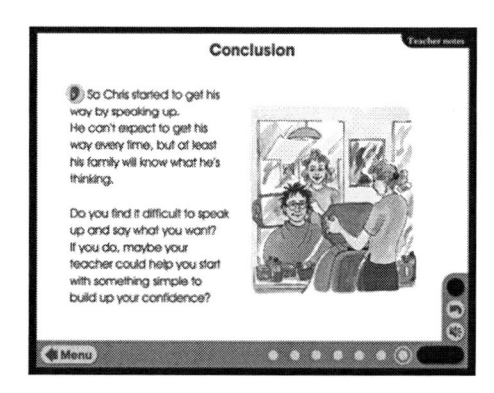

Resources for: 'Learning to Speak Up'

## 2. 'MAKING DECISIONS TOGETHER' INTERACTIVE ACTIVITY TEACHER NOTES

This is a bespoke activity in which different groups of people (families, friends etc) have to reach compromises on what to do together, where to go, which film to see and so on.

After each choice, to add an element of interest, there is a randomly generated outcome.

### RELATES TO: 'MOVING ON TO COLLEGE' PAGES 2, 4 & 8
### LEVEL: 1-2

#### OBJECTIVES

Students learn:

- That we all have different likes and dislikes and we must respect this.
- How to try for a satisfactory solution that everyone can accept.
- The need for compromise.
- The importance of fairness.

#### FOLLOW-UP ACTIVITIES

- Give students similar situations to the activity which they have to resolve in small groups using first, second and third preferences.
- Students recall situations that weren't resolved fairly.
- Various role-play situations from the book or elsewhere.

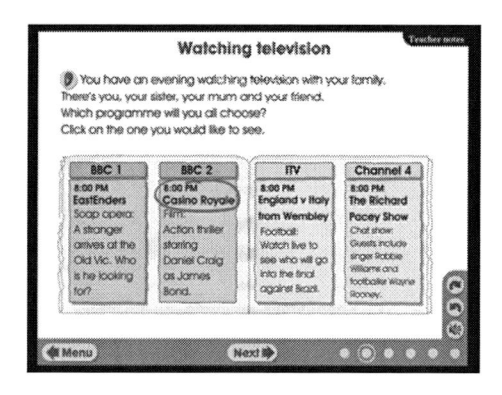

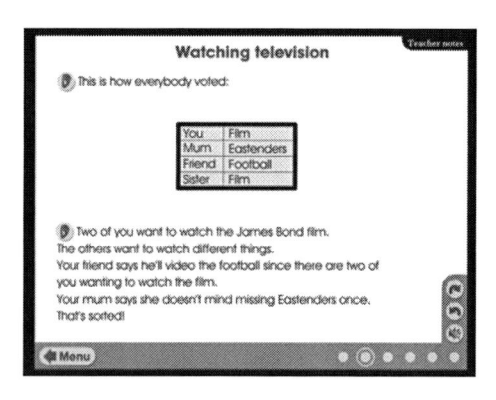

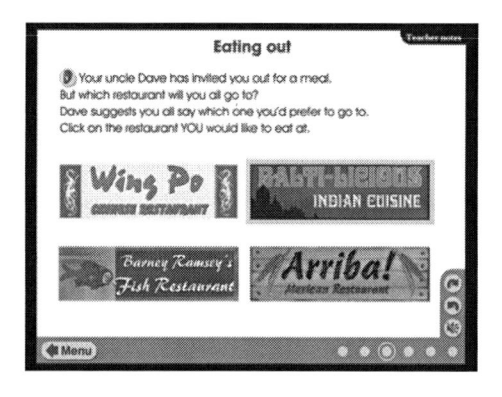

# RESOURCE SHEETS

**You may copy these sheets freely for use in your school/college.**

There are nine resource sheets which relate specifically to *Learning to Speak Up*:

### THE BOOK AND ACTIVITIES FEEDBACK SHEET
Students write a sentence or two giving their views on the book and activities they've just tackled and think about anything they might have learned.

### STUDENT RECORD SHEET
A record sheet for the teacher to record the various activities undertaken by the student in this part of the topic, and the level achieved.

### HOW WELL DID YOU READ?
Ten simple true or false questions related to the text.

### COVER SHEET
A sheet for students to decorate, and use as a cover for their resource sheets folder.

### WORDS AND PICTURES
Match ten words with illustrations from the book.

### PICTURE SEARCH
Search the book for six illustrations, then write a sentence about each of them.

### KEYWORD FLASHCARDS
Sixteen story-related words taken from the text. These need to be printed onto card and cut up.

### WORDSEARCH
Ten key words chosen from the flashcards.

### SPOT THE DIFFERENCE
An illustration from the book with six details changed.

# The book and activities feedback sheet

1. Say what you thought of the book.
(Could you read it and understand it? Did you find it interesting? A bit? Was it boring? Did you like any of the illustrations? Which one(s)?)

..................................................................................................................

..................................................................................................................

..................................................................................................................

2. Say what you thought of the interactive activities.
(Did you find them easy to use? Did you enjoy any of them? Which one(s)?)

..................................................................................................................

..................................................................................................................

..................................................................................................................

3. Say if you learned anything from either.

..................................................................................................................

..................................................................................................................

..................................................................................................................

..................................................................................................................

© SEN Press 2008. All rights reserved.

# Student record sheet
## Learning to Speak Up

............................................................has,

- Read the text - with help/without help

- Made a contribution to the discussion - yes/no

- Completed the *How well did you read*? exercise - with help/without help
  Score:....................

- Tackled the 16 flashcards and achieved this score:......................

- Completed these interactive activities
  - Speaking up
  - Making decisions together

- Completed these additional tasks or activities:
  - ..............................................................................................
  - ..............................................................................................
  - ..............................................................................................

- Completed these other resource sheets:
  - Book and activities feedback sheet
  - Wordsearch
  - Word puzzle
  - Spot the difference
  - Cover drawing

- Other related challenges undertaken and lessons learned:
  - ..............................................................................................
  - ..............................................................................................
  - ..............................................................................................

© SEN Press 2008. All rights reserved.

# How well did you read?

Five of these are TRUE, and five are FALSE

| | | |
|---|---|---|
| 1. | Chris's mum has a job. | TRUE / FALSE |
| 2. | He has an older sister called Kate. | TRUE / FALSE |
| 3. | The family has a black cat. | TRUE / FALSE |
| 4. | Chris wanted a Chinese meal. | TRUE / FALSE |
| 5. | Chris's dad wanted to watch a film on ITV. | TRUE / FALSE |
| 6. | Chris liked Manchester United. | TRUE / FALSE |
| 7. | He wanted his mum to buy him some leather shoes. | TRUE / FALSE |
| 8. | He is 16. | TRUE / FALSE |
| 9. | He liked listening to local radio. | TRUE / FALSE |
| 10. | He chose his own hairstyle in the end. | TRUE / FALSE |

© SEN Press 2008. All rights reserved.

# Learning to Speak Up

Name _____

Class _____

© SEN Press 2008. All rights reserved.

# Words and pictures

- Match up the words with their pictures. Draw a line between each pair

cactus plant

steering wheel

high-heeled shoes

a framed picture of Manchester United

TV remote control

personal stereo

A-Z street atlas

computer keyboard

bookcase

box of tissues

© SEN Press 2008. All rights reserved.

Resources for: 'Learning to Speak Up'

# Picture search

- Look for each of these illustrations.
- Write down which pages you found them on.
- Try putting each word into a sentence.

I found a **cactus plant** on page _____

*write your* cactus plant *sentence here*

I found a **steering wheel** on page _____

*write your* steering wheel *sentence here*

I found some **high-heeled shoes** on page _____

*write your* high-heeled shoes *sentence here*

I found a **framed picture of Manchester United** on page _____

*write your* framed picture of Manchester United *sentence here*

I found a **TV remote control** on page _____

*write your* TV remote control *sentence here*

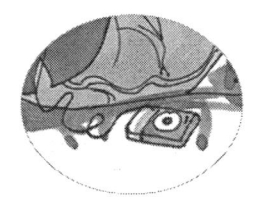

I found a **personal stereo** on page _____

*write your* personal stereo *sentence here*

© SEN Press 2008. All rights reserved.

# Key words flashcards

| | |
|---|---|
| choose | take-away |
| pizza | Chinese |
| change | programme |
| clothes | shoes |

© SEN Press 2008. All rights reserved.

# Key words flashcards

| | |
|---|---|
| trainers | radio |
| BBC1 | ITV |
| EastEnders | good value |
| hairdresser | embarrassing |

© SEN Press 2008. All rights reserved.

# Wordsearch

Search for the hidden words from the lists in this grid.

| p | o | y | k | s | g | b | r | b | m | s | s |
|---|---|---|---|---|---|---|---|---|---|---|---|
| r | w | y | c | h | i | n | e | s | e | h | c |
| f | h | o | q | o | i | e | h | q | y | i | h |
| t | o | r | c | e | f | r | a | d | i | o | a |
| c | h | o | o | s | e | n | e | v | r | u | n |
| o | h | r | i | n | c | u | e | d | n | k | g |
| p | p | l | c | l | o | t | h | e | s | p | e |
| i | i | g | r | x | u | k | o | b | q | j | m |
| z | j | p | z | t | a | k | e | a | w | a | y |
| z | d | t | r | a | i | n | e | r | s | n | b |
| a | i | a | h | t | o | n | b | l | e | o | l |
| c | o | p | r | o | g | r | a | m | m | e | m |

choose  
take-away  
pizza  
Chinese  
change  

programme  
clothes  
shoes  
trainers  
radio

# Spot the difference

Can you spot the six differences in the pictures. Ring them on the picture on the right.

# RESOURCES FOR 'SHOPPING FOR MUM'

**'SHOPPING FOR MUM'**

**EVERYDAY CHALLENGES SERIES**

**LEVEL: 1-2**

**READING AGE: 5.8 YEARS**

**16 PAGES**

**213 WORDS**

## KEY THEMES

A small shopping task undertaken independently.

Identifying different everyday products on the shelves.

Noticing price differences.

The influences of advertising and marketing.

Peer pressure.

Coping with the unexpected.

Overspending and what to do.

Handling money.

## THE NARRATIVE

Rachel finds a note from her mum when she gets back from school. Will she go down to the local store? She has been left a small shopping list of five items and a £5 note. Everything seems to be going well until she reaches the checkout. It's at this point that she discovers that she's overspent by 10p. What can she do?

The book offers an opportunity to take students through what is involved in shopping for more than one item and the possible pitfalls. It describes a typical shopping task, but not one that the majority of special school students have yet achieved. For them this challenge lies in the future.

# PAGE BY PAGE NOTES FOR THE TEACHER

## SHOPPING FOR MUM: PAGE 1

- Ask students what happens when they get home from school. Do they have keys to get in? Are they alone? What do they usually do?

## SHOPPING FOR MUM: PAGES 2-3

- Talk about leaving notes for each other. When might this be done? Have any of the students done it? When? Why?

## SHOPPING FOR MUM: PAGES 4-5

- Study the two page illustration for information: when is the store open? Does it sell newspapers? Could you buy a lottery ticket here?

## SHOPPING FOR MUM: PAGES 6-7

- Look at the variety of bread to choose from.
- Discuss differences and student preferences.

Resources for: 'Shopping for Mum'

## SHOPPING FOR MUM: PAGES 8-9

- Why does Rachel buy both?
- Which is the more expensive, the apple or the banana?
- If Rachel had been asked to buy a whole kilo of bananas, how would she know how many to get?
- How many students eat fruit regularly?

## SHOPPING FOR MUM: PAGES 10-11

- Look at the choice of shampoo available and the different needs each meets.
- Have students thought why well-known brands are generally more expensive than the others?
- Why do they think Rachel chose *Chic* shampoo? Will she be thinking about the price?

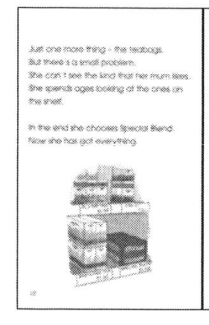

## SHOPPING FOR MUM: PAGES 12-13

- Talk about the unexpected and what to do if the store doesn't have what's on your shopping list.

## SHOPPING FOR MUM: PAGES 14-15

- If you're able and IT-minded, you might consider explaining simply how stock items are scanned in and out of a store, what barcodes are for, the need for stock control etc.

## SHOPPING FOR MUM: PAGE 16

- *Don't* solve Rachel's problem here. Move on to the activity "Being Careful with Your Money" - see page 74 - which takes students through each step that Rachel has taken and hints at possible solutions.

Resources for: "Shopping for Mum"

# INTERACTIVE ACTIVITIES

There are two interactive activities that develop key themes in the narrative. They are designed for use both on whiteboards and individual PCs.

## 1. 'CHOICES IN THE SHOPS' INTERACTIVE ACTIVITY TEACHER NOTES

The activity comprises questions for the student about different brands of the same commodity (bread, shampoo, tea,). Students learn to look at the wording on labels and to spot small differences.

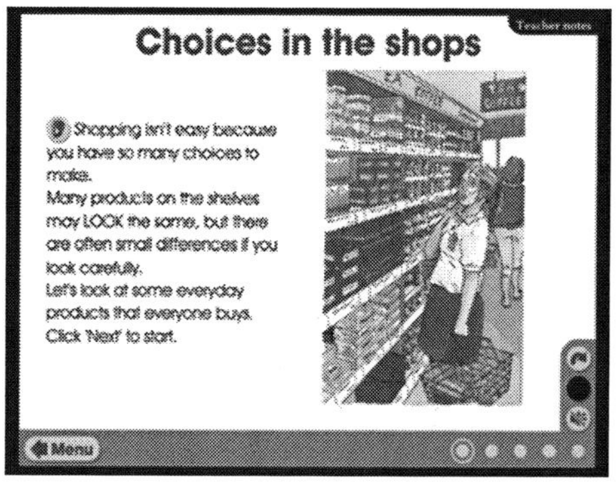

### RELATES TO: 'SHOPPING FOR MUM' PAGES 7, 9-13
### LEVEL: 1-2

### OBJECTIVES

Students learn:
- To examine the range of goods on a particular shelf and their differences.
- Make more informed choices by studying the labels.
- To be aware of price differences.
- Not be influenced by fancy packaging.

### FOLLOW-UP ACTIVITIES

- Students visit a local supermarket with a number of tasks, eg to compare prices of Heinz baked beans with the supermarket's own brand; find the cheapest/most expensive washing up liquid and so on.
- Students go to the supermarket with a small shopping list of items for a cookery lesson and a calculator, and try to keep within a particular budget.
- A simple exercise to locate a number of different, specialised items eg an anti-dandruff shampoo, a slimmer's loaf, a particular brand of tea.

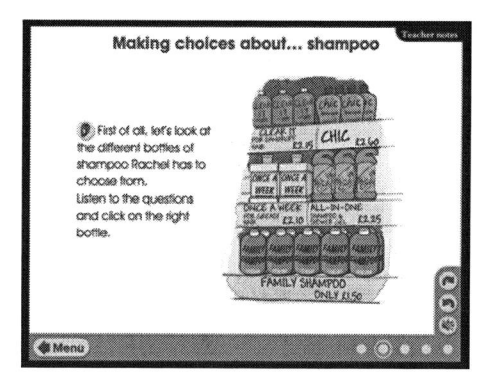

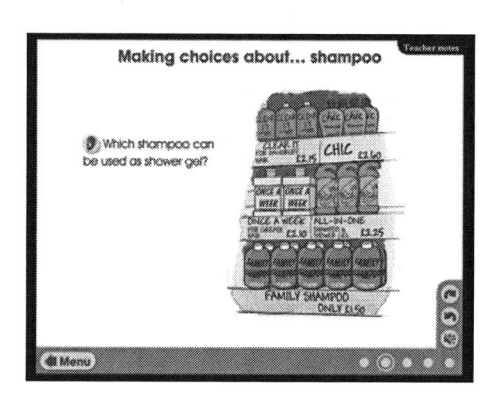

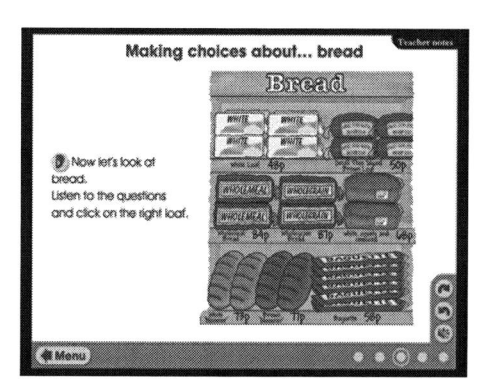

Resources for: 'Shopping for Mum'

## 2. 'BEING CAREFUL WITH YOUR MONEY' INTERACTIVE ACTIVITY TEACHER NOTES

This activity reviews each step Rachel took in the shop; then students are given an opportunity to change or exchange certain items in order to help Rachel to stay within her £5 budget.

### RELATES TO: 'SHOPPING FOR MUM' PAGES 2, 16
### LEVEL: 1-2

#### OBJECTIVES

Students learn:
- That they need to be aware of the price of the item they are buying.
- That they will pay more for TV- marketed brands in fancy packaging.
- Not to panic if they don't have enough money to pay – there is often a simple solution.

#### FOLLOW-UP ACTIVITIES

- Role play – at the checkout. Not having enough money.
- Experiment with cheap and expensive shampoo or washing up liquid in school, and establish if there's any difference in quality or value for money. Is the most expensive the best?
- Talk about what is *good value*.
- Get students to explain why they think we pay more for well-known brands on TV.

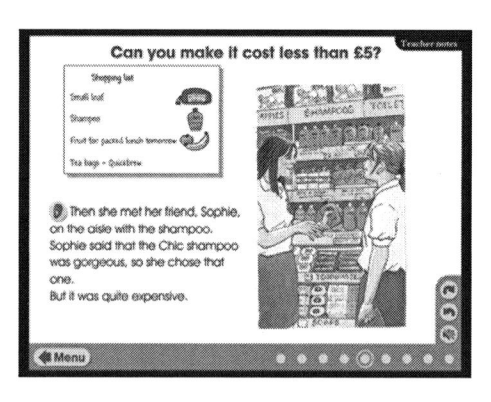

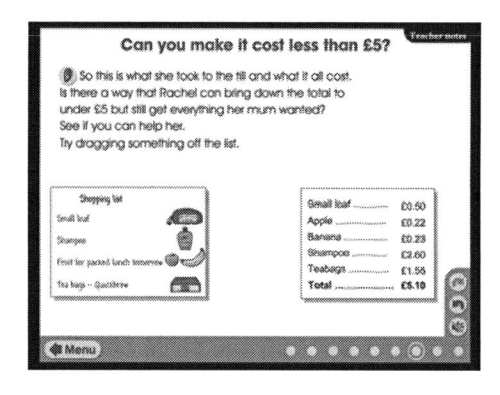

# RESOURCE SHEETS

**You may copy these sheets freely for use in your school/college.**

There are nine resource sheets which relate specifically to *Shopping for Mum:*

### THE BOOK AND ACTIVITIES FEEDBACK SHEET
Students write a sentence or two giving their views on the book and activities they've just tackled and think about anything they might have learned.

### STUDENT RECORD SHEET
A record sheet for the teacher to record the various activities undertaken by the student in this part of the topic, and the level achieved.

### HOW WELL DID YOU READ?
Ten simple true or false questions related to the text.

### COVER SHEET
A sheet for students to decorate, and use as a cover for their resource sheets folder.

### WORDS AND PICTURES
Match ten words with illustrations from the book.

### PICTURE SEARCH
Search the book for six illustrations, then write a sentence about each of them.

### KEYWORD FLASHCARDS
Sixteen shopping-related words taken from the text. These need to be printed onto card and cut up.

### WORDSEARCH
Ten key words chosen from the flashcards.

### SPOT THE DIFFERENCE
An illustration from the book with six details changed.

Resources for: 'Shopping for Mum'

# The book and activities feedback sheet

1. Say what you thought of the book.

(Could you read it and understand it? Did you find it interesting? A bit? Was it boring? Did you like any of the illustrations? Which one(s)?)

..............................................................................................................................

..............................................................................................................................

..............................................................................................................................


2. Say what you thought of the interactive activities.

(Did you find them easy to use? Did you enjoy any of them? Which one(s)?)

..............................................................................................................................

..............................................................................................................................

..............................................................................................................................


3. Say if you learned anything from either.

..............................................................................................................................

..............................................................................................................................

..............................................................................................................................

..............................................................................................................................

© SEN Press 2008. All rights reserved.

# Student record sheet
## **Shopping for Mum**

............................................................has,

- Read the text - with help/without help

- Made a contribution to the discussion - yes/no

- Completed the *How well did you read?* exercise - with help/without help
  Score:....................

- Tackled the 16 flashcards and achieved this score:.......................

- Completed these interactive activities
    - Choices in the shops
    - Being careful with your money

- Completed these additional tasks or activities:
    - ...............................................................................
    - ...............................................................................
    - ...............................................................................

- Completed these other resource sheets:
    - Book and activities feedback sheet
    - Wordsearch
    - Word puzzle
    - Spot the difference
    - Cover drawing

- Other related challenges undertaken and lessons learned:
    - ...............................................................................
    - ...............................................................................
    - ...............................................................................

© SEN Press 2008. All rights reserved.

Resources for: 'Shopping for Mum'

# How well did you read?

Five of these are TRUE, and five are FALSE

| | | |
|---|---|---|
| 1. | Rachel had her own house key. | TRUE / FALSE |
| 2. | She found a note from her dad. | TRUE / FALSE |
| 3. | The note told Rachel to buy a takeaway meal. | TRUE / FALSE |
| 4. | There were five things on the shopping list. | TRUE / FALSE |
| 5. | She chose a small white loaf. | TRUE / FALSE |
| 6. | She chose an apple and a banana. | TRUE / FALSE |
| 7. | She met her friend Sophie. | TRUE / FALSE |
| 8. | She bought her mum's favourite tea. | TRUE / FALSE |
| 9. | There was a queue at the checkout. | TRUE / FALSE |
| 10. | Her bill came to £5.10. | TRUE / FALSE |

© SEN Press 2008. All rights reserved.

# Shopping for Mum

Name _____

Class _____

© SEN Press 2008. All rights reserved.

# Words and pictures

- Match up the words with their pictures.
  Draw a line between each pair

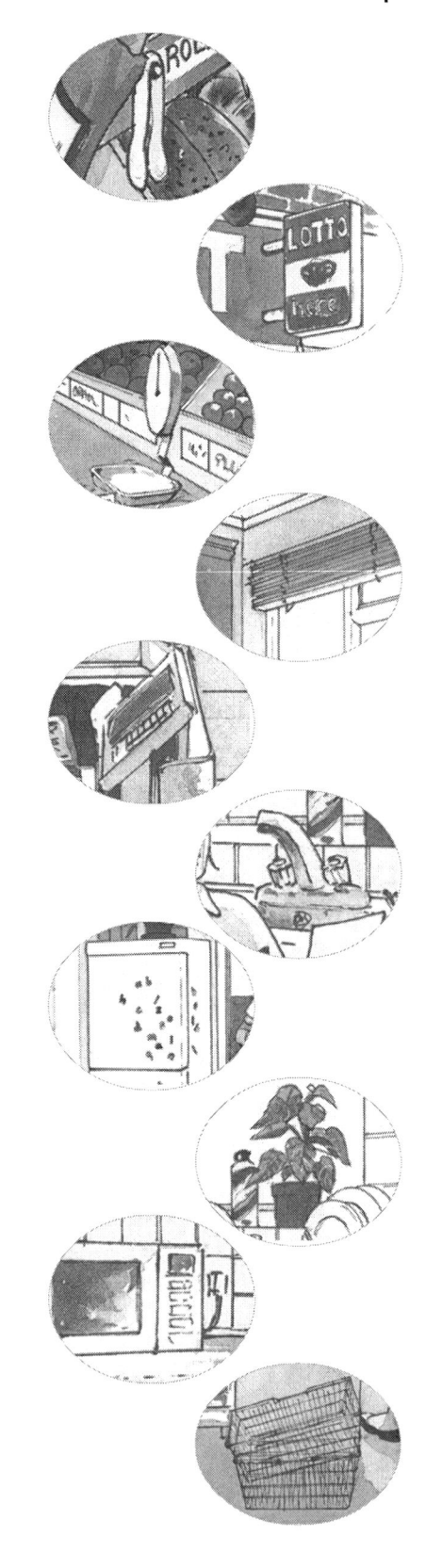

microwave oven

checkout till

pot plant

lottery ticket sign

fridge freezer

food tongs

wire baskets

mixer taps

weight scales

window blind

© SEN Press 2008. All rights reserved.

Resources for: "Shopping for Mum"

# Picture search

- Look for each of these illustrations.
- Write down which pages you found them on.
- Try putting each word into a sentence.

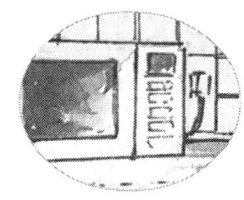

I found a **microwave oven** on page _____

*write your* microwave oven *sentence here*

I found a **checkout till** on page _____

*write your* checkout till *sentence here*

I found a **pot plant** on page _____

*write your* pot plant *sentence here*

I found a **lottery ticket sign** on page _____

*write your* lottery ticket sign *sentence here*

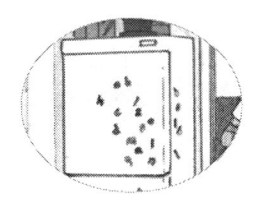

I found a **fridge freezer** on page _____

*write your* fridge freezer *sentence here*

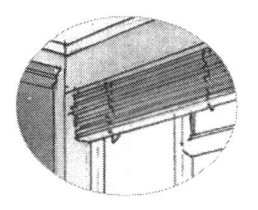

I found a **window blind** on page _____

*write your* window blind *sentence here*

© SEN Press 2008. All rights reserved.

## Key words flashcards

| | |
|---|---|
| kitchen | loaf |
| shampoo | fruit |
| basket | banana |
| apple | decide |

# Key words flashcards

| | |
|---|---|
| shelf | checkout |
| corner shop | shopping list |
| packed lunch | tea bags |
| receipt | problem |

Resources for: 'Shopping for Mum'

# Wordsearch

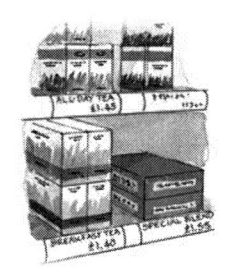

Search for the hidden words from the lists in this grid.

| a | p | p | l | e | y | t | h | v | q | b | r |
|---|---|---|---|---|---|---|---|---|---|---|---|
| v | k | c | f | w | b | n | l | e | b | v | m |
| n | s | h | a | m | p | o | o | b | m | o | n |
| m | i | b | q | b | l | n | a | i | p | s | b |
| d | e | c | i | d | e | y | f | t | n | g | a |
| h | d | k | i | t | c | h | e | n | s | t | n |
| v | w | o | u | l | m | p | f | i | h | f | a |
| f | i | e | e | j | b | a | s | k | e | t | n |
| r | p | b | c | t | s | m | n | j | l | o | a |
| u | w | t | z | m | b | e | n | y | f | v | n |
| i | y | p | h | n | y | k | j | u | t | o | u |
| t | h | c | h | e | c | k | o | u | t | q | a |

kitchen          banana
loaf             apple
shampoo          decide
fruit            shelf
basket           checkout

© SEN Press 2008. All rights reserved.

Resources for: 'Shopping for Mum'

# Spot the difference

Can you spot the six differences in the pictures. Ring them on the picture on the right.

# RESOURCES FOR 'SHOPPING FOR CLOTHES'

**'SHOPPING FOR CLOTHES'**

**EVERYDAY CHALLENGES SERIES**

**LEVEL: 1-2**

**READING AGE: 5.9 YEARS**

**16 PAGES**

**378 WORDS**

## KEY THEMES

Developing personal taste and style.

Making independent choices.

Clothes for special occasions.

Seeking value for money.

Planning a shopping trip.

Comparing goods in more than one shop.

Being careful with money.

'Sales' and 'bargains'.

## THE NARRATIVE

Anna wants a new top for her school leavers' party. Linda, her foster mum, helps her to plan their shopping trip, and is there to advise, but she makes it clear that Anna must make the final choice.

The book looks at some of the main points that young people need to be taken through when choosing clothes for themselves.

Resources for: "Shopping for Clothes"

# PAGE BY PAGE NOTES FOR THE TEACHER

## SHOPPING FOR CLOTHES: PAGE 1

- Do any of the students live with foster-parents? If appropriate, ask them to explain the term.
- School leavers' parties.

## SHOPPING FOR CLOTHES: PAGES 2-3

- Linda is planning the shopping trip for Anna's benefit. She wants Anna to think about which shops might be suitable, how much she has to spend etc before they set off.
- How many of the group have money saved up? Is it for something special? Do they get pocket money or an allowance each week? Money at Christmas or on birthdays?

## SHOPPING FOR CLOTHES: PAGES 4-5

- How many students know their size for anything they are wearing? See the "What's My Size?" Interactive Activity (page 89) for a close look at sizes, male and female. It is to be done in pairs.
- Can Anna afford to buy one of these tops for £19.99?

## SHOPPING FOR CLOTHES: PAGES 6-7

- Linda is demonstrating the importance of taking time when choosing clothes – trying them on and looking at the labels.
- Ask the students what would happen if they tried to wash a top that stated "Dry clean only".

# Resources for: 'Shopping for Clothes'

## SHOPPING FOR CLOTHES: PAGES 8-9

- Draw the students' attention to Linda who is carefully steering Anna into making the decisions through carefully chosen questions.

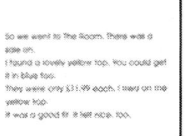

## SHOPPING FOR CLOTHES: PAGES 10-11

- Get the students to talk about where they buy their clothes. Girls *and* boys. Do they buy off the peg from one place or try several places? Have they benefited from a sale?

## SHOPPING FOR CLOTHES: PAGES 12-13

- Ask the students if *they* think the yellow top was the best choice.
- Talk about colours that go well together, both orthodox and unorthodox.

## SHOPPING FOR CLOTHES: PAGES 14-15

- Look at widely used marketing terms like 'sale', 'bargain', 'buy one, get one free' which are beguiling and sometimes make people buy more than they originally intended.

## SHOPPING FOR CLOTHES: PAGE 16

- An opportunity to point out how we all appreciate small presents that show generosity and thoughtfulness. Many would have kept both tops for themselves.

Resources for: "Shopping for Clothes"

# INTERACTIVE ACTIVITIES

There are two interactive activities that develop key themes in the narrative. They are designed for use both on whiteboards and individual PCs.

## 1. 'WHAT'S YOUR SIZE?' INTERACTIVE ACTIVITY TEACHER NOTES

This is a measuring activity to be undertaken by the students *in pairs*. They will be shown on the CD how to make a number of key measurements for different types of clothes and record these using their keyboards. At the end they will be given a table of their sizes (generated by the program using measurement criteria from a reputable mail order catalogue!) which they can print out.

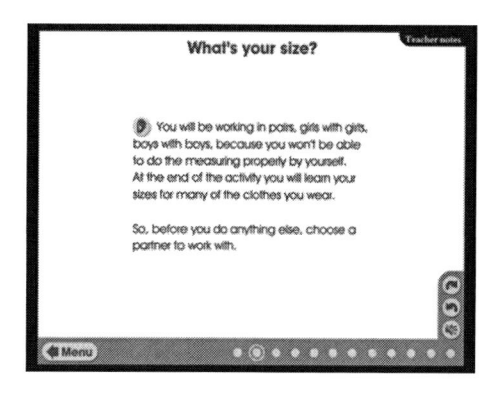

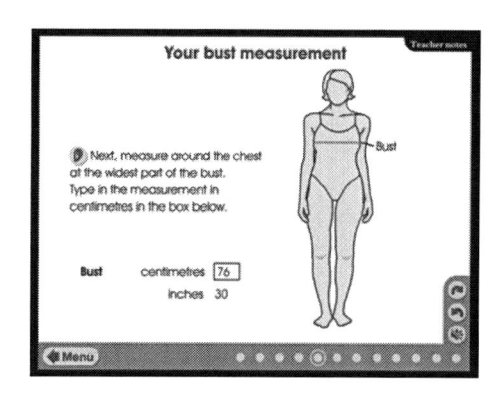

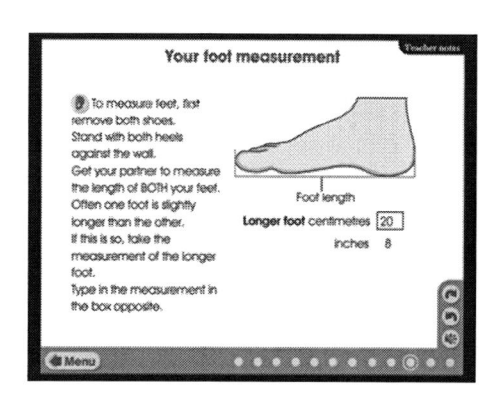

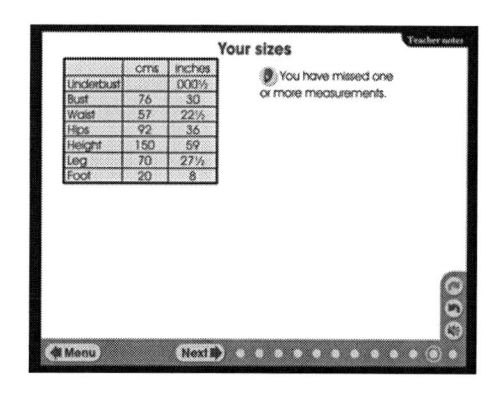

### RELATES TO: 'SHOPPING FOR CLOTHES' PAGES 4-7
### LEVEL: 1-2

### OBJECTIVES

Students gain:
- A relevant experience in measuring.
- A record of their different clothes sizes.
- An understanding of how these have been arrived at.
- Information helpful to them in choosing clothes for themselves.

### FOLLOW-UP ACTIVITIES

- Students take home their list of sizes for parent/guardian to check.
- If appropriate, collate some of the figures to establish the tallest down to the shortest in the group; the boy with the biggest/smallest collar size and so on.

# Resources for: 'Shopping for Clothes'

## 2. "TIPS FOR CLOTHES SHOPPING' INTERACTIVE ACTIVITY TEACHER NOTES

This activity comprises ten simple, right-or-wrong-type questions from the story – five to be answered "right" and five "wrong". The student will listen to ten remarks made by Anna about clothes shopping in the form of speech bubbles and will have to decide which are sensible and which aren't.

### RELATES TO: 'SHOPPING FOR CLOTHES' PAGES 1-16
### LEVEL: 1-2

### OBJECTIVES

Students better understand:
- What is involved in shopping for clothes.
- Some marketing language, such as SALE and BARGAIN.
- The importance of patience and not buying the first thing they see or like.
- The importance of trying on clothes and making sure they fit.
- Clothes labels and the information they give.
- The importance of being careful with their money.
- The importance of making their own choices and developing their own tastes in clothes.

### FOLLOW-UP ACTIVITIES

- Visit clothes shops when SALES are on to witness what goes on.
- Talk about returning goods: good reasons for doing so, the procedure, keeping receipts, money-back or exchange etc.
- Get students to talk about occasions in which they or their parents returned goods and why this was. Clothes that didn't fit?
- Talk about washing machine disasters – dyes and stains, shrinkage etc.
- Various role-play situations in a clothes shop.

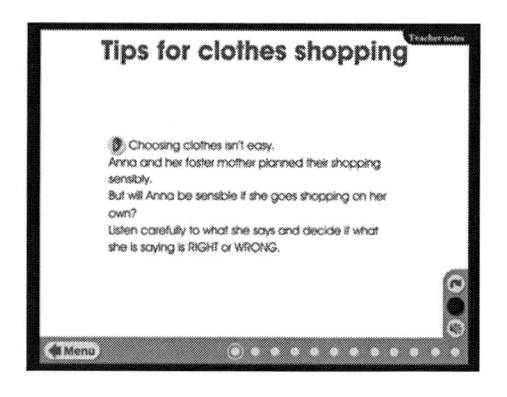

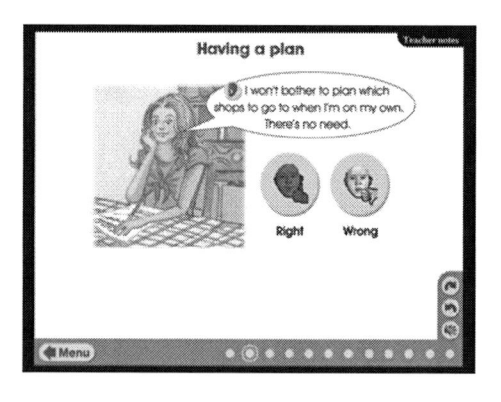

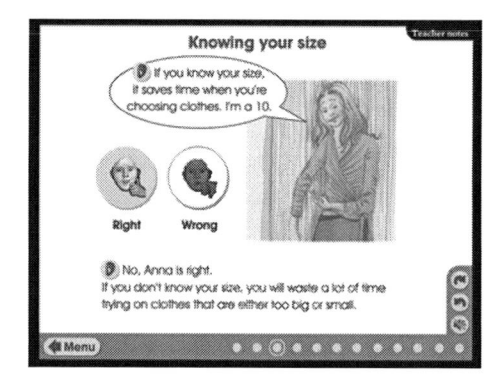

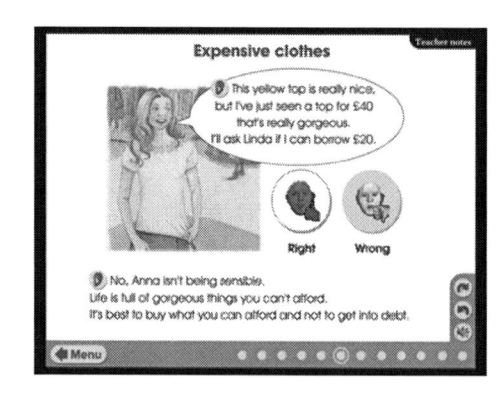

# RESOURCE SHEETS

**You may copy these sheets freely for use in your school/college.**

There are nine resource sheets which relate specifically to *Shopping for Clothes:*

## THE BOOK AND ACTIVITIES FEEDBACK SHEET
Students write a sentence or two giving their views on the book and activities they've just tackled and think about anything they might have learned.

## STUDENT RECORD SHEET
A record sheet for the teacher to record the various activities undertaken by the student in this part of the topic, and the level achieved.

## HOW WELL DID YOU READ?
Ten simple true or false questions related to the text.

## COVER SHEET
A sheet for students to decorate, and use as a cover for their resource sheets folder.

## WORDS AND PICTURES
Match ten words with illustrations from the book.

## PICTURE SEARCH
Search the book for six illustrations, then write a sentence about each of them.

## KEYWORD FLASHCARDS
Sixteen shopping-related words taken from the text. These need to be printed onto card and cut up.

## WORDSEARCH
Ten key words chosen from the flashcards.

## SPOT THE DIFFERENCE
An illustration from the book with six details changed.

Resources for: 'Shopping for Clothes'

# The book and activities feedback sheet

1. Say what you thought of the book.

(Could you read it and understand it? Did you find it interesting? A bit? Was it boring? Did you like any of the illustrations? Which one(s)?)

...................................................................................................................

...................................................................................................................

...................................................................................................................

2. Say what you thought of the interactive activities.

(Did you find them easy to use? Did you enjoy any of them? Which one(s)?)

...................................................................................................................

...................................................................................................................

...................................................................................................................

3. Say if you learned anything from either.

...................................................................................................................

...................................................................................................................

...................................................................................................................

...................................................................................................................

© SEN Press 2008. All rights reserved.

Resources for: "Shopping for Clothes"

# Student record sheet
## Shopping for Clothes

..................................................has,

- Read the text - with help/without help

- Made a contribution to the discussion - yes/no

- Completed the *How well did you read?* exercise - with help/without help
  Score:..................

- Tackled the 16 flashcards and achieved this score:.....................

- Completed these interactive activities
    - What's your size?
    - Tips for clothes shopping

- Completed these additional tasks or activities:
    - ...............................................................................
    - ...............................................................................
    - ...............................................................................

- Completed these other resource sheets:
    - Book and activities feedback sheet
    - Wordsearch
    - Word puzzle
    - Spot the difference
    - Cover drawing

- Other related challenges undertaken and lessons learned:
    - ...............................................................................
    - ...............................................................................
    - ...............................................................................

© SEN Press 2008. All rights reserved.

Resources for: 'Shopping for Clothes'

# How well did you read?

Five of these are TRUE, and five are FALSE

| | | |
|---|---|---|
| 1. | Anna had foster parents. | TRUE / FALSE |
| 2. | Her leavers' party was on a Saturday evening. | TRUE / FALSE |
| 3. | She had £30 saved up. | TRUE / FALSE |
| 4. | She wanted a new top for the party. | TRUE / FALSE |
| 5. | She was a Size 10. | TRUE / FALSE |
| 6. | Linda said she would pay for the top. | TRUE / FALSE |
| 7. | There was a SALE on at Clothes Junction. | TRUE / FALSE |
| 8. | She bought a yellow top for herself. | TRUE / FALSE |
| 9. | Linda chose Anna's top for her. | TRUE / FALSE |
| 10. | Anna got a blue top free and gave it to Linda. | TRUE / FALSE |

© SEN Press 2008. All rights reserved.

# Shopping for Clothes

Name _____

Class _____

© SEN Press 2008. All rights reserved.

Resources for: 'Shopping for Clothes'

# Words and pictures

- Match up the words with their pictures.
  Draw a line between each pair

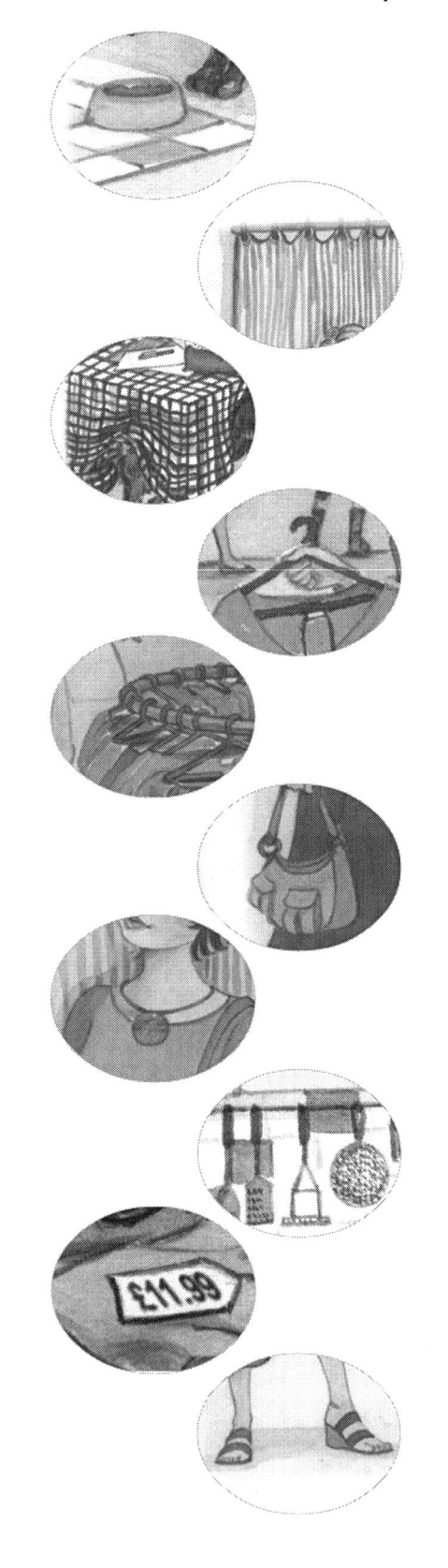

**clothes rail**

**necklace**

**clothes hanger**

**handbag**

**cat's food bowl**

**pair of sandals**

**changing room curtain**

**price tag**

**checked table cloth**

**kitchen utensils**

© SEN Press 2008. All rights reserved.

Resources for: "Shopping for Clothes"

# Picture search

- Look for each of these illustrations.
- Write down which pages you found them on.
- Try putting each word into a sentence.

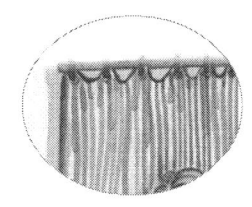

I found a **clothes rail** on page _____

*write your* clothes rail *sentence here*

I found a **necklace** on page _____

*write your* necklace *sentence here*

I found a **cat's food bowl** on page _____

*write your* cat's food bowl *sentence here*

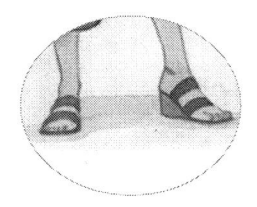

I found a **pair of sandals** on page _____

*write your* pair of sandals *sentence here*

I found a **price tag** on page _____

*write your* price tag *sentence here*

I found some **kitchen utensils** on page _____

*write your* kitchen utensils *sentence here*

© SEN Press 2008. All rights reserved.

# Key words flashcards

| | |
|---|---|
| skirt | shopping |
| choose | money |
| clothes | expensive |
| cheap | size |

# Key words flashcards

| | |
|---|---|
| price | tight |
| sleeve | dry clean |
| label | wash |
| sale | jumper |

© SEN Press 2008. All rights reserved.

# Wordsearch

Search for the hidden words from the lists in this grid.

| r | d | w | b | o | i | u | p | r | i | c | e |
|---|---|---|---|---|---|---|---|---|---|---|---|
| s | s | k | i | r | t | h | b | r | k | n | m |
| w | h | q | u | e | i | p | l | b | x | e | s |
| t | o | h | c | h | e | a | p | j | n | x | f |
| h | p | s | k | t | h | o | b | n | a | p | l |
| u | p | r | r | h | c | h | o | o | s | e | b |
| b | i | v | i | j | c | l | k | y | u | n | m |
| p | n | v | s | i | z | e | t | m | b | s | i |
| o | g | o | q | y | j | b | e | o | e | i | y |
| b | r | t | i | g | h | t | x | n | q | v | k |
| w | o | h | b | v | j | o | m | e | b | e | n |
| c | l | o | t | h | e | s | u | y | t | k | l |

skirt

shopping

choose

money

clothes

expensive

cheap

size

price

tight

© SEN Press 2008. All rights reserved.

Resources for: 'Shopping for Clothes'

# Spot the difference

Can you spot the six differences in the pictures. Ring them on the picture on the right.